Historical and Cultural Dictionaries of Asia
edited by Basil C. Hedrick

1. *Saudi Arabia,* by Carroll L. Riley. 1972.
2. *Nepal,* by Basil C. and Anne K. Hedrick. 1972.
3. *The Philippines,* by Ester G. and Joel M. Maring. 1973.
4. *Burma,* by Joel M. and Ester G. Maring. 1973.
5. *Afghanistan,* by M. Jamil Hanifi. 1976.
6. *Thailand,* by Harold Smith. 1976.
7. *Vietnam,* by Danny J. Whitfield. 1976.
8. *India,* by George Kurian. 1976.

edited by Carroll L. Riley

9. *The Sultanate of Oman and the Emirates of Eastern Arabia,* by John Duke Anthony. 1976.

Historical and Cultural Dictionary of the SULTANATE OF OMAN and the EMIRATES OF EASTERN ARABIA

by

JOHN DUKE ANTHONY

with contributions and assistance from
John Peterson and Donald Sean Abelson

Historical and Cultural Dictionaries of Asia, No. 9

The Scarecrow Press, Inc.
Metuchen, N.J. 1976

Library of Congress Cataloging in Publication Data

Anthony, John Duke.
Historical and cultural dictionary of the Sultanate of Oman and the Emirates of eastern Arabia.

(Historical and cultural dictionaries of Asia ; no. 9)
Bibliography: p.
1. Persian Gulf States--Dictionaries and encyclopedias. 2) Oman--Dictionaries and encyclopedias. I. Peterson, John, 1947- II. Abelson, Donald S. III. Title: Historical and cultural dictionary of the Sultanate of Oman... IV. Series: Historical and cultural dictionaries of Asia series ; no. 9.
DS247.A13A68 953'.5'003 76-42216
ISBN 0-8108-0975-3

Manufactured in the United States of America

TO THE PEOPLE OF EASTERN ARABIA

EDITOR'S FOREWORD

John Duke Anthony was born and grew up in Richmond, Va. He holds degrees from the Virginia Military Institute, the Graduate School of Foreign Service of Georgetown University and the Johns Hopkins University School of Advanced International Studies (SAIS) in Washington, where he is a member of the faculty of the Center for Middle Eastern Studies. Over the past fifteen years, Dr. Anthony has travelled extensively in Middle Eastern countries, including Iran, Turkey and most of the Arabic-speaking states. During the 1970s he has conducted several years of research in the Arabian Peninsula and Lower Gulf states on problems related to political and socio-economic change in the region. He is the author of Arab States of the Lower Gulf: People, Politics, Petroleum (1975) and the editor and co-author of The Middle East: Oil, Politics and Development (1975). He has contributed to a number of other works, among which are: U.S. Interests in and Policy Toward the Persian Gulf (1972); New Perspectives on the Persian Gulf (1973); and The Persian Gulf: Money, Arms, Politics and Power (1975). In addition to teaching courses on the Arabian Peninsula and the Gulf states at SAIS, he is assistant editor of the Middle East Journal. During 1975-76 he served as chairman, Near East/North Africa Studies, Foreign Service Institute, U.S. Department of State.

John Peterson obtained his bachelor's and master's degrees from the University of Arizona. He is a Ph.D. candidate at SAIS. Mr. Peterson's doctoral dissertation, "Oman in the Twentieth Century: Foundations of a Developing State," is based on extensive archival and field research carried out during 1974 and 1975 in Great Britain and Oman. Mr. Peterson works as a research assistant in the Center for Middle East Studies at SAIS and as a librarian with the George Camp Keiser Library of the Middle East Institute in Washington. Donald Sean Abelson holds a master's degree in international economics and Middle East studies from SAIS, where he conducted research on the Arabian Peninsula in the Center for Middle East Studies. Upon graduation in 1975, he joined the U.S. Department of Commerce.

The ten states covered in this dictionary are vitally important to the oil-hungry Western world and Japan, and this dictionary fills a vacuum of knowledge on this area of immense strategic significance.

Carroll L. Riley
Professor and Associate Director
Southern Illinois University
Museum and Art Galleries

INTRODUCTION

This dictionary is designed to help fill a long-standing deficiency in the literature on the people and history of the Sultanate of Oman and the nine emirates of Eastern Arabia. The reasons for the growing importance of these states in recent years are obvious: they line the littoral of one of the world's most strategic sea lanes and they lie astride or adjacent to substantial sources of oil and gas. Yet despite the greatly enhanced significance of these states in global affairs, most outsiders know very little about the numerous forces, issues, personalities and historical events that have shaped the distinctive character of their people and culture. The information, description and analysis included herein therefore represent an initial attempt at correcting this deficiency.

Eastern Arabia, as defined herein, encompasses the area covered by al-Bahrayn, Qatar, the seven member states of the United Arab Emirates and the Sultanate of Oman. Entries on other geographical areas that have had an important effect on Eastern Arabia at some point in time have also been included, such as Iran, al-Kuwayt, Saudi Arabia and Zanzibar. The word "Gulf," when standing alone, refers to the body of water variously known as the Arabian or Persian Gulf.

A system of cross-references has been included in the body of most entries in the form of all capital letters used for the appropriate names or phrases. Entries for prominent Arab figures are to be found under the individual's proper name and not under generic/family/tribal names (e.g., under "'Abd Allah bin Humayd al-Salimi," not "al-Salimi, 'Abd Allah bin Humayd" or "Bin Humayd, 'Abd Allah").

An attempt has been made to follow the Library of Congress transliteration system for Arabic words, but with several modifications. These include the elimination of all diacritical markings except "'" (for the 'ayn and hamza), and the substitution of "dh" for "ẓ" in order to avoid confusion for the unfamiliar reader. For the same reason, a few place names already established in Western usage have been left as they are commonly found, such as Muscat instead of Masqat, Sharjah instead of al-Shariqah, Abu Dhabi instead of Abu Ẓabi, emirates instead of amirates, Nasser for Nasir, and Koran for Qur'an.

The preparation of this dictionary was facilitated by numerous persons and institutions. H. M. Sultan Qabus Al Bu Sa'id, Ruler of Oman, made it possible for some of the field work for the study to take place through a generous supportive grant and the extension of transportation, accommodation and other kinds of logistical assistance. Additional assistance was provided by H. E. Faysal bin 'Ali Al Bu Sa'id, H. E. Ahmad Macki, H. E. Nasir bin Seif Al Bu 'Ali, Sadek Suleiman, Ahmad Raidan and 'Abd al-'Aziz bin Muhammad al-Ruwas of the Sultanate of Oman; H. E. Seif Ghobash, H. E. Saeed Ghobash, H. E. Mahdi Tajir, Ibrahim Ibrahim, Muhammad Darweesh Bin Karam, and Saeed al-Shamsy of the United Arab Emirates; H. E. Jasim bin Hamad Al Thani, H. E. Nasir bin Khalid Al Thani, and Daud Fanus of Qatar; and John Townsend, Malcolm Dennison, Marje and Harvey Doorenbas, William Duff, N. Elam, Muhammad Lisanul Haq, David and Frauke Heard-Bey, Edward Henderson, J. C. Kelly, Sir William Luce, Colin Maxwell, Frederick McEldowney, George Nafieh, Julius Paxton, Bill Peyton, Anthony Reeve, Mervyn Underhill, John Ward and Robin Young. To each of these individuals, the Arabian American Oil Company, Petroleum Development (Oman) Ltd., the Arabian Mission in Matrah, Oman, of the Reformed Church of America and, especially, the governments of the Eastern Arabian states, the contributors acknowledge their deep appreciation.

The task of preparing the manuscript for the press would not have been completed but for the typing and other administrative assistance of Miss Eileen Donlin, the editing skills of Ms. Darcie Ann Bundy, and the strong support of Dean Robert E. Osgood and Prof. Majid Khadduri, all of the Johns Hopkins University School of Advanced International Studies in Washington, and Mr. William Sands, whose good offices made it possible for the project to be undertaken.

J. D. A.

THE DICTIONARY

ADMA see ABU DHABI MARINE AREAS

ADPC see ABU DHABI PETROLEUM CO.

ALBA (Aluminum Bahrayn). A firm established under the State of al-BAHRAYN Development Bureau's plan to diversify the industrial composition of the Bahrayni economy. The company is a consortium of American, French, British and Swedish firms as well as the Bahrayn government. Production, begun in 1970, soon reached 120,000 tons of aluminum per year. In the mid-1970s, there were plans to enlarge the facility and to expand its operations to include secondary aluminum industries, such as those in the manufacture of window frames, powder and other products. The energy fuel stock for the plant is derived from natural gas, a by-product of petroleum production, which was formerly flared at the well head and hence lost to commercial use. As the first enterprise to demonstrate successfully the role of natural gas in diversifying one of the Eastern Arabian economies, ALBA has become something of a showpiece in the GULF area.

ANM see ARAB NATIONALISTS MOVEMENT

'ABD ALLAH BIN HUMAYD al-SALIMI (d. 1920). Blind IBADI theologian of the late 19th and early 20th centuries. He was instrumental in resurrecting the Ibadi IMAMATE in 1913 with SALIM BIN RASHID al-KHARUSI as IMAM. His book, <u>Tuhfat al-A'yan fi Sirat Ahl 'Uman</u>, provides a detailed history of OMAN from the beginning of the age of ISLAM until the early 20th century. His son, Muhammad bin 'Abd Allah, was mentioned as a possible candidate in the 1954 election for Imam, and wrote <u>Nahdat al-A'yan bi-Hurriyat 'Uman</u>, a continuation of his father's history up to the death of Imam MUHAMMAD BIN 'ABD ALLAH al-KHALILI in

1954, and 'Uman: Ta'rikh Yatakallim, a defense of the 1950s Imamate of GHALIB BIN 'ALI al-HINA'I.

'ABD ALLAH BIN QASIM AL THANI. Ruler of the State of QATAR (r. 1913-1949) with whom Great Britain signed a Treaty of Protection in 1916. During his rulership, petroleum was discovered in Qatar. He was noted for his long and patriarchical reign and his voluntary abdication of the rulership to his son, 'ALI BIN 'ABD ALLAH.

'ABRIYYIN see 'IBRIYYIN

ABU DHABI [Abu Ẓabi]. The largest of the seven member states of the UNITED ARAB EMIRATES (UAE). The majority of the population resides in Abu Dhabi Town (founded ca. 1761) although al-LIWA and al-'AYN are also population centers. The area of the shaykhdom is approx. 26,000 miles and the estimated population in the mid-1970s was 235,662, of which probably no more than 50,000 were indigenous to the state, the rest being immigrants from other parts of the Arab world, Europe, Iran and the Indian subcontinent who had been attracted by the booming oil-based economy. The major tribe is the Al Bu FALAH section of the Bani YAS and the ruling dynasty is from the Al NUHAYYAN family.

Abu Dhabi Town, the capital of the UAE, is located on an island and in the mid-1970s had an estimated population of 80,000. The town was little more than a fishing village prior to 1966 when Shaykh ZAYID BIN SULTAN AL NUHAYYAN replaced his brother SHAKHBUT and, with the help of vast oil revenues, began to develop it along with other areas in the shaykhdom.

ABU DHABI MARINE AREAS LTD. (ADMA). The first oil-producer in the State of ABU DHABI. ADMA was formed as a consortium between the Anglo-Iranian Oil Company (AIOC; later British Petroleum or BP), with a two-thirds interest, and Compagnie Française des Pétroles (CFP), with one-third. In 1953 ADMA received an off-shore concession from Abu Dhabi. In 1958 oil was discovered at Umm al-Shayf field (ca. 75 miles northwest of A.D. Town). Production began in 1962 after a 20-mile underwater pipeline was laid to DAS ISLAND where a major terminal was built. A second field was subsequently discovered (al-Zakum). The company also operates the concession for al-Bunduq field, which lies between Abu Dhabi and QATAR and from which Abu Dhabi and Qatar divide revenues equally.

After part of ADMA's territory had been relinquished a second offshore concession was granted in 1967 to Abu Dhabi Oil Company (Japan), comprised of three Japanese companies (Maruzen Oil Co., Daikyo Oil Co., and Nippon Mining Co.). This company discovered oil in 1970 and subsequently began exports from Halat al-Mubarraz Island (ca. 22 miles from the mainland, west of Abu Dhabi Town and south of ADMA's al-Zakum field). Two other offshore concessions were granted to European and Japanese consortia in the early 1970s.

ABU DHABI PETROLEUM COMPANY (ADPC). The major onshore concession operator in the State of ABU DHABI. It was originally known as Petroleum Development (Trucial Coast) Ltd. (PDTC) when, as a subsidiary of the Iraq Petroleum Co. (IPC), it received a concession for the shaykhdom in 1939. Although active exploration began in 1949, oil was not discovered until 1960; export began in December 1963. Production is centered around Habshan, Shamis and Asab in the western portion of the shaykhdom and pipelines connect the fields to the tanker terminal further west at Jabal al-Dhannah. The name PDTC was changed to Abu Dhabi Petroleum Co. in 1962 and headquarters were consolidated in Abu Dhabi Town during 1965-1966. Previously the company's headquarters had been in al-BAHRAYN, with field offices at Tarif on the coast between Jabal al-Dhannah and Abu Dhabi Town. ADPC ownership is vested in the Abu Dhabi government, British Petroleum (BP), Royal Dutch Shell, Compagnie Française des Pétroles, the Near East Development Corp. (equally owned by Standard of New Jersey and Mobil) and Partex (the Gulbenkian interests).

A number of areas relinquished by ADPC were regranted in 1965 as a new concession to a consortium comprised of Phillips Petroleum Co., the American Independent Oil Co. (Aminoil) and the Italian AGIP. In 1968, another concession covering territory relinquished from ADPC was granted to Middle East Oil Co., which is owned by Mitsubishi Oil Development Co. of Japan.

ABU MUSA ISLAND. A small island strategically located at the eastern end of the Gulf near the entrance to the Strait of HORMUZ. The island was administered by

Great Britain and the State of SHARJAH until its occupation by Iranian naval forces in November of 1971. The prior agreement of Shaykh KHALID BIN MUHAMMAD al-QASIMI (Ruler of Sharjah 1965-1972) to this occupation was a factor in his assassination during an unsuccessful coup attempt in Sharjah in January 1972. The island has been mined since prehistoric times for its red oxide.

ADAM. Village settlement located on the WADI HALFAYN in the western part of al-SHARQIYYAH province in OMAN. Most of Adam's inhabitants belong to the Al Bu SA'ID tribe and the present ruling family of the Sultanate of OMAN claims the village as its ancestral home.

al-'ADHAYBAH (AZAIBA). A village on the BATINAH Coast of OMAN about ten miles west of MATRAH, which served as operations center for PETROLEUM DEVELOPMENT (OMAN) LTD. from the early 1950s until the discovery of oil in the late 1960s. For a number of years al-'Adhaybah had the only airstrip in the MUSCAT/Matrah area.

'ADNANI-YAMANI DIVISION. A supposedly racial division dating from the first and second waves of prehistoric Arab immigration to Eastern Arabia. The first group was the Yamani ("Yemeni" or Qahtani) which came from the Yemen in the south and settled in the OMAN province in the interior of geographical Oman. Centuries later, the 'ADNANI (or Nizari) tribes came into the area from the north, settling in al-DHAHIRAH province (to the north of Oman province), and along the TRUCIAL COAST (as well as al-BAHRAYN and QATAR). Although this division is allegedly along racial lines (the Yamani tribes claiming to be the "pure" Arabs, while the northern tribes are known as "musta'aribah" or of less purely Arab origins), the division is in fact more political than anything else. In Oman, the division has been buttressed by the GHAFIRI and HINAWI tribal confederations which, to some degree, are based upon these lines.

AHMAD BIN 'ALI AL THANI. Ruler of the State of QATAR from 1960 to 1972. Under his reign, the first municipality was established in 1968 at al-DAWHAH. Like his father and predecessor as Ruler, Shaykh 'ALI BIN 'ABD ALLAH, Ahmad preferred to spend his time in traditional and in literary pursuits. His rulership was marked by considerable economic development and administrative reform but also by scandal and financial extravagance (Ahmad spent much of his time at retreats in Switzerland and elsewhere). Part of the reason for his ouster from power in 1972 was his refusal to establish a State Advisory Council as called for in the Temporary Constitution of 1970. He was replaced by his cousin, KHALIFAH BIN HAMAD.

AHMAD BIN IBRAHIM AL BU SA'ID. The Omani Minister of the Interior for Sultan SA'ID BIN TAYMUR from 1939 to 1970. The nephew of Imam 'AZZAN BIN QAYS AL BU SA'ID (d. 1871), Ahmad became in 1916 the independent ruler of al-RUSTAQ, a town which was traditionally held independently of MUSCAT by the descendants of a collateral branch of the family of the Sultans of OMAN. A year later, however, Ahmad was forced to retreat to al-HAZM by the forces of the Imam SALIM BIN RASHID al-KHARUSI. His need to call for assistance from Sultan TAYMUR BIN FAYSAL helped to unify the two branches of the AL BU SA'ID dynasty. Ahmad later was appointed wali (governor) of several towns on the BATINAH Coast, particularly al-SUWAYQ and remained in this post until he was appointed Minister of the Interior in 1939. Following the reassertion of Sultanate control over the interior of Oman in the mid-1950s, Ahmad was put in charge of the government's relations with the tribal shaykhs of the area. In that position, he functioned as the shaykhs' principal link to the Sultan (and vice versa), who was in residence in faraway SALALAH, the capital of DHUFAR Province.

AHMAD BIN MAJID see SHIHAB al-DIN AHMAD BIN MAJID

AHMAD BIN MUHAMMAD al-HARITHI. TAMIMAH (paramount shaykh) of the HIRTH tribe in al-SHARQIYYAH province in OMAN from 1956 to 1971. Ahmad was arguably the last representative of the powerful tribal leaders who had dominated the politics of interior Oman for centuries. He is the son of Muhammad bin 'Isa, who served as the Hirth's tamimah for a brief period during the late 1940s. Ahmad's claim to succeed his father following the latter's premature death (ca. 1950) was circumvented by his uncle, SALIH BIN 'ISA. Consequently, Ahmad established an alliance with Sultan

SA'ID BIN TAYMUR. When Salih bin 'Isa fled the country in 1956, along with other supporters of Imam GHALIB, who opposed the Sultan, the Sultan appointed Ahmad as tamimah of the Hirth, temporary wali of NIZWA--the most important town of interior Oman--and basically relied upon him from that point onwards as his representative in the interior. Further to solidify what was essentially a pragmatic political alliance, the Sultan arranged for his only son, Heir Apparent QABUS BIN SA'ID, to become engaged to one of Ahmad's daughters in early 1970. Fulfillment of the contract was forestalled, however, by the coup d'état of July 1970 by which Qabus became Sultan. Unable or unwilling to reconcile himself to the new order of increased administrative control over the interior by the Sultanate government, Ahmad was placed under house arrest in MUSCAT in 1971.

AHMAD BIN RASHID al-MU'ALLA. Ruler of the State of UMM al-QAYWAYN since 1929 and paramount shaykh of the Al 'Ali tribe. Among the heads of individual states in the UNITED ARAB EMIRATES (UAE), only Shaykh RASHID BIN HUMAYD al-NU'AYMI of 'AJMAN has ruled longer (since 1928). Because of his advanced age in the mid-1970s, Shaykh Ahmad was the least active Ruler in the UAE, leaving many public functions to his son, Crown Prince Rashid.

AHMAD BIN SA'ID AL BU SA'ID. The first Al Bu Sa'id Imam of OMAN (r. 1744-1783). He was first wali (governor) of SUHAR for the YA'ARIBAH dynasty when the Persians invaded Oman in 1737. After several unsuccessful sieges of Suhar, the Persians eventually reached an agreement with Ahmad whereby he would serve as wali for them. Despite this supposed understanding, Ahmad led the opposition to the Persians and finally evicted them from the forts of MUSCAT in 1744. He was then elected Imam (religious leader) and made his capital at al-RUSTAQ where he died and was buried in 1783.

'AJMAN. One of the seven members of the UNITED ARAB EMIRATES (UAE). 'Ajman was recognized by the British as an independent shaykhdom in the GENERAL TREATY OF PEACE in 1820, although it has long been overshadowed by its larger and more prosperous neighbors, DUBAY and SHARJAH. The present Ruler, Shaykh RASHID BIN HUMAYD al-NU'AYMI, has been in power since 1928. The Nu'aymi ruling family is part of the larger NA'IM tribe centered around al-BURAYMI Oasis, which straddles the border dividing the UAE State of ABU DHABI from the SULTANATE OF OMAN. 'Ajman is the smallest of the Eastern Arabian emirates, with a territory of approximately 100 sq. miles and an estimated population in the mid-1970s of 21,566, most of whom live in 'Ajman Town on the coast, although there are several enclaves in the interior in the HAJAR mountains.

AKHDAR see al-JABAL al-AKHDAR

AL. Arabic word meaning family. Often used in Eastern Arabia as part of the name of a distinguished family, dynasty or tribe (such as the Al NUHAYYAN family or the Al Bu SHAMIS tribe). The word should not be confused with the article al- (meaning "the"), generally used in place names but at times as part of a tribal name as well (such as the city of al-MANAMAH and al-HAWASINAH tribe). In this dictionary, an entry containing "al" or "al-" will be found under the proper part of the name.

'ALAYAH--SIFALAH. Arabic terms meaning "upper" and "lower" respectively and used to refer to the two distinct areas frequently found in Omani towns. Generally, one section will be occupied by tribes belonging to the northern Arab race (known as 'ADNANI or Nizari) while the other quarter will be inhabited by tribes belonging to the southern Arab race (YAMANI or Qahtani). Further, if the 'alayah quarter belongs to GHAFIRI tribes (one side of the basic dichotomy dominating Omani tribal politics), the sifalah quarter will often belong to HINAWI tribes (or vice versa). In towns where these divisions occur, the wali (governor) will often occupy a fort that is situated in a neutral position. Most of these forts are well placed should there be need to separate the different factions. Prominent examples are in the town of NIZWA where a broad wadi (watercourse) divides the walled sections, IZKI, and SAMA'IL. In the latter village, al-'Alayah is separated from al-Sifalah by several miles.

ALBUQUERQUE, AFFONSO DA see PORTUGUESE IN EASTERN ARABIA

'ALI, BANI BU (singular: 'Alawi). One of the two most important tribes of the JA'LAN province of OMAN, the other being the Bani Bu HASAN. As the latter are HINAWI in politics, the Bani Bu 'Ali are GHAFIRI as well as being Hanbali SUNNIS. Their capital is at Bilad Bani Bu 'Ali, with another major settlement at al-'Ayqah section of the coastal town of SUR. A joint Sultanate-British expedition led against Bilad Bani Bu 'Ali in 1820 (to punish the tribe for its acts of piracy) ended in disaster for the invader. The defeat was avenged, however, by a much larger army the following year. The Bani Bu 'Ali later became one of the most important tribal supporters of the AL BU SA'ID sultans until disputes arose over the issue of customs at Sur and the tribe sought to enlist SAUDI support for its own customs house at al-'Ayqah. Until as recently as the July 1970 coup d'état the Bani Bu 'Ali, largely because of their long tradition as being among the most independent-minded of any people in Eastern Arabia, were one of the few tribes who refused to have anything to do with the Sultanate, the IMAMATE or PETROLEUM DEVELOPMENT (OMAN) LTD.

'ALI BIN 'ABD ALLAH AL THANI. Ruler of the State of QATAR from 1949 to 1960, he ascended to the rulership when his father, 'ABD ALLAH BIN QASIM, voluntarily abdicated. His reign marked the inception of a modern administrative structure, with financial and military advisors and a Director of Government. 'Ali was more inclined to traditional and intellectual pursuits than the day-to-day administration of government and eventually abdicated in favor of his son, AHMAD BIN 'ALI.

'ALIM see 'ULAMA'

ALUMINUM BAHRAYN see ALBA

AMIR (plural: 'umara'). Arabic title with the various meanings of tribal chief, commander, or prince. In Eastern Arabia it has been used by the rulers of the Gulf states (i. e., al-BAHRAYN, QATAR and the member states of the UNITED ARAB EMIRATES) and on occasion also by various tribal shaykhs in OMAN who have sought to increase their influence.

'AMIRI see 'AWAMIR

ARAB NATIONALISTS MOVEMENT (ANM). A moderately

leftist political organization begun in the late 1940s in Lebanon by George Habash and other Palestinians and which at one time followed the ideas of Jamal 'Abd al-Nasir. A branch of the ANM was subsequently established in al-KUWAYT, and a number of students from Eastern and Southern Arabia became ANM members or supporters. ANM activists were involved in several of the strikes and labor demonstrations that occurred in al-BAHRAYN during the late 1950s and on various occasions during the 1960s. The organization was also one of the principal founders of the National Liberation Front in what used to be known as the Crown Colony of Aden and the Aden Protectorate (now the People's Democratic Republic of the Yemen) and was a prime supporter of the DHUFAR REBELLION in its early stages. Although many of the initial leaders of the Dhufar Liberation Front (DLF) were ANM members, leadership of the insurrection subsequently passed to more radical Dhufaris of Marxist persuasion. A large number of the earlier, more moderate rebel leaders defected to the new regime that came to power in the Sultanate of OMAN in July 1970.

ARABIAN [Persian] GULF. The body of water separating the Arabian Peninsula from the southwest Asian mainland. Its northern source is the Shatt al-'Arab (formed by the merger of the Tigris and Euphrates Rivers) in Iraq and it empties into the Gulf of OMAN at the Strait of HORMUZ. The Gulf lies in a northwesterly-southeasterly direction and is approximately 570 miles long and from 125 to 275 miles wide. The waterway, which is very shallow and reaches a maximum depth of approximately 500 feet, is noted for its variety of sea life, its pearling banks and underwater petroleum deposits, and its role as one of the most strategically important maritime arteries in the world. The littoral states of the Gulf are Iran, Iraq, al-KUWAYT, SAUDI ARABIA, QATAR, the seven member states of the UNITED ARAB EMIRATES, and the Sultanate of OMAN. The BAHRAYN archipelago lies just off the western coast of the Qatar Peninsula and forms a separate state. Major coastal settlements include: Bandar 'Abbas, BUSHIRE, al-KUWAYT, al-DAMMAM, Ra's Tanurah, al-MANAMAH, al-DAWHAH, ABU DHABI, DUBAY, SHARJAH, 'AJMAN, UMM al-QAYWAYN, RA'S al-KHAYMAH and KHASAB.

ARABIAN MISSION. A missionary organization of the Reformed Church of America (a branch of the Dutch Reformed Church). The Mission was organized in August 1889 and its first missionaries were James Cantine and Samuel ZWEMER. Missions were eventually established in MUSCAT/MATRAH, al-BAHRAYN, al-KUWAYT and al-Basrah (Iraq). Unsuccessful attempts were made to extend the Mission's evangelist activities into the interior of OMAN and the Eastern Province (al-Hasa) of what is now SAUDI ARABIA. As conversion of Muslims to Christianity was frowned upon, the activities of the missions eventually concentrated on providing medical care and education. Until comparatively recent times, the Mission was one of the few institutions to offer these activities in Eastern Arabia.

AUCHER-ELOY, PIERRE MARTIN see OMAN

al-'AWALI. A town of central al-BAHRAYN Island located in the desert approximately 12 miles south of al-MANAMAH. It has been the headquarters of BAHRAIN PETROLEUM CO. (BAPCO) since the early 1930s.

'AWAMIR (singular: 'Amiri). A large tribe dispersed over a substantial segment of Eastern Arabia. About half of the tribe has settled in OMAN, mainly around the town of Qalah (a few miles south of IZKI in OMAN province and where the tamimah or paramount shaykh for the 'Awamir's settled sections lives) and on the BATINAH Coast near al-SIB. The badu (nomadic) sections range from al-DHAFRAH (in ABU DHABI) and al-BURAYMI (on the Abu Dhabi-Oman border) in the north to the Hadramawt (the area in the eastern part of the People's Democratic Republic of Yemen from which the tribe is believed to have originated). As a whole, the 'Awamir are SUNNI and GHAFIRI. The tribe's settled sections have long been at odds with the Bani RUWAHAH tribe in Oman province and also with the HAWASINAH on the Batinah; in addition, nomadic 'Awamir have often been in feud with the DURU', an important tribe of interior Oman. The 'Awamir are one of four tribes that commonly range across al-RUB' al-KHALI desert (the others being the Murrah, the Manahil and the Rawashid).

AWLAD (singular: walad). Arabic word meaning sons, frequently used in the name of a tribal subdivision or to denote the male offspring of a notable individual. For entries which begin with awlad, see rest of name (e.g., KHALILI, Awlad).

al-'AYN. The major settlement of al-BURAYMI Oasis. The name is also used by many in ABU DHABI to refer to that part of the oasis which belongs to the State of Abu Dhabi (including five other villages besides al-'Ayn). In 1955 al-Buraymi was recaptured from SAUDI ARABIA, which, in support of its claim to sovereignty over the nine villages in the immediate vicinity, had stationed a police detachment in the area since 1952. Al-'Ayn has been the focus of considerable socio-economic development since the mid-1960s, because of the emirate's impressive revenues from oil. The town is linked to the capital (Abu Dhabi Town) by a 90-mile divided highway. In the mid-1970s, it boasted a Hilton hotel, cinemas, hospitals, electricity, and many other modern amenities. By contrast, the portion of the oasis (three villages out of nine) under the sovereignty of the Sultanate of OMAN, though also undergoing numerous developments, still retained much of its traditional character. For many people al-'Ayn is also a favorite retreat from the heat of Abu Dhabi Town on the coast; this is due to its many date gardens and much lower level of humidity. The present Ruler of Abu Dhabi, Shaykh ZAYID BIN SULTAN AL NUHAYYAN, served as wali (governor) of al'Ayn for twenty years prior to becoming Ruler in 1966.

AZAIBA see al-'ADHAYBAH

'AZZAN BIN QAYS AL BU SA'ID. IMAM of Oman (r. 1868-1871) with his capital at MUSCAT. 'Azzan was descended from a collateral branch of the Al Bu SA'ID family of Sultans, a line which traditionally provided the rulers of al-RUSTAQ and which was semi-independent of the Sultans in Muscat. Backed by SALIH BIN 'ALI (tamimah or paramount shaykh of the HIRTH tribe), 'Azzan was elected Imam by a confederation of mostly HINAWI tribes, and in 1868 conquered Muscat, driving the Sultan, Salim bin Thuwayni, into exile. Primarily through the influence of his chief adviser, SA'ID BIN KHALFAN al-KHALILI, and the MUTAWWI' (religious leader) faction, the Government of India (and particularly, the Political Resident in the Persian Gulf, Lewis PELLY) perceived the new Muscat government as being xenophobic and religiously bigoted, and thus withheld the ZANZIBAR SUBSIDY.

Without this subsidy, the regime was quickly bankrupted and unable to maintain the loyalty of the tribes. Consequently, two contenders to the Muscat throne appeared: the old Sultan Salim (who was discouraged by the Government of India and also lacked significant tribal support); and Salim's uncle, Turki bin Sa'id. The latter individual rallied the tribes of the SHARQIYYAH province to his side and, with the tacit support of Pelly, managed to conquer Muscat, whereupon he killed both 'Azzan and Sa'id bin Khalfan al-Khalili. Although at the time his reign began, the mutawwi's were in a powerful position, 'Azzan had gradually come to make his own moderation felt. He had also been noted for his military prowess, as evidenced by the extension of his control to many areas of Oman that had been independent of Muscat since the middle of Sultan SA'ID BIN SULTAN's reign of 1807-1856. 'Azzan's downfall was due largely to the hostility of Pelly who believed that 'Azzan's regime was little more than yet another manifestation of the MUWAHHIDUN (Wahhabism). Despite this setback, 'Azzan's descendants continued to rule al-Rustaq independently of the Sultans in Muscat until it was captured by the forces of Imam SALIM BIN RASHID al-KHARUSI in 1917.

- B -

BAPCO see BAHRAIN PETROLEUM CO.

BBME see BRITISH BANK OF THE MIDDLE EAST

BADGER, the Rev. GEORGE P. A 19th-century chaplain to the Government of Bombay and an Arabic and Persian scholar, Badger served on the Coghlan Commission of 1860-61 (which ratified the separation of ZANZIBAR from OMAN) and the Frere Mission of 1873 (which investigated the problem of slavery in Zanzibar). He served as interpreter for the Government of Bombay and translated from Arabic into English a number of works, the most important being the classical Arabic history of Oman, the *Kashf al-Ghummah*, the English version of which appeared under the title *History of the Imams and Seyyids of 'Oman by Salil ibn Razik* (London, 1871).

BADU [Bedouin]. Arabic term for nomad, often used in contrast with HADR (settled). By long tradition the badu of Eastern Arabia have occupied the marginally productive land between the seacoasts and the deserts of the interior where their livelihoods are centered on goatherding and camel breeding. Some badu tribes (such as sections of the Bani YAS or the DURU') have an established territory (DIRAH), and they frequently own date gardens in OASES to which they return at intervals during harvest time. Sections of these tribes have become settled; important examples include the ruling families of al-BAHRAYN, QATAR, ABU DHABI and DUBAY, who have settled along the GULF. Other badu tribes such as the 'AWAMIR and MANASIR are not yet bound to settlements and continue to range widely across the Arabian Peninsula. These tribes, which are usually small in number, often regard themselves as the purest of all Arabs and tend to scorn townspeople. As vast oil revenues rapidly accrue to the states of Eastern Arabia, the always-precarious economic position of the badu is becoming increasingly less feasible. Consequently, attempts are being made, particularly in Qatar and Abu Dhabi, to settle them and provide them with training and equipment in agriculture or other vocations. Wilfred THESIGER has written a very valuable account of badu life in his book Arabian Sands.

al-BAHARINAH (singular: Bahrani). Arabic term used in al-BAHRAYN to distinguish its original inhabitants, who are a mixture of Arab and Persian blood and SHI'I in religion. In OMAN the term is used somewhat more loosely, referring to Ithna'ashari Shi'is in general, particularly those with an Iraqi or Persian background. The Baharinah of al-Bahrayn constitute approximately half of the inhabitants and were an important factor in Iran's long-standing claim to the Bahrayn Islands (relinquished in 1970). In Oman, the Baharinah tend to be merchants, often wealthier and more educated than the general populace. Even so, owing largely to their religious position as Shi'is in a situation where the ruling family subscribes to the IBADI sect of Islam, relatively few among them have been able to achieve important government positions.

BAHARNA see al-BAHARINAH

BAHLA. One of the major towns of OMAN province, Bahla lies approximately 20 miles to the northwest of NIZWA. It was the capital of the IMAMATE during the Al NABAHINAH dynasty, which ranged from the 12th to the 17th centuries. The town of Jabrin, which also served briefly in the 17th century as the capital of the Imamate, is located in the Wadi Bahla near the town of

Bahla. While Bahla's once impressive fortress is nowadays in ruins, that of Jabrin ranks as the best preserved Omani fortification. Also, near Bahla is the first agricultural experimental station in Oman, established ca. 1960. Bahla is also known throughout Eastern Arabia and the GULF as a center of pottery and of superstition.

BAHRAIN PETROLEUM CO. (BAPCO). The only oil producer within the State of al-BAHRAYN. BAPCO is a subsidiary of the American firm Caltex, with Standard Oil of California and a later partner, Texaco, each holding 50 per cent interests. The company was registered in 1930 in Canada to overcome obstacles to non-British oil companies in the area and began production in 1932. Headquarters are located at al-'AWALI south of the capital of al-MANAMAH. Due to its nearly half a century of production, BAPCO has exhausted much of Bahrayn's oil supply and nowadays an underwater pipeline from the Eastern Province (al-Hasa) of nearby SAUDI ARABIA provides much of the crude oil processed in BAPCO's refinery. See also OIL EXPLORATION.

al-BAHRAYN. An independent state and archipelago of 30 islands on the southern side of the Gulf near the QATAR Peninsula. The islands encompass approximately 250 square miles and in the mid-1970s had an estimated population of 250,000. The state is ruled by a shaykh of the Al KHALIFAH family, who came to the islands in the 18th century from the village of al-ZUBARAH on the west coast of the Qatar Peninsula. Al-Bahrayn was a British-protected state from the mid-19th century until August 1971. At that time Great Britain terminated its special treaty relationship with al-Bahrayn by which it had been responsible for the shaykhdom's defense and foreign relations. Having thereby achieved its full independence, al-Bahrayn became a member of the United Nations and the Arab League. From 1948 to 1971 the island state was the seat of British power in the Gulf. That approximately half of its population belongs to the SHI'I sect of Islam (the other half is SUNNI, the predominant sect on the Arab side of the Gulf) and that individuals of Iranian nationality or ancestral origin compose a substantial portion of the state's population, are factors which reinforced an Iranian claim to sovereignty over the islands until as recently as 1970.

The capital and largest town is al-MANAMAH,

located at the northern end of al-Bahrayn Island, which is the largest in the archipelago and approximately 35 miles long. The second largest town is al-MUHARRAQ, located on an island of the same name that is connected to al-Manamah by a causeway. Al-Bahrayn was the first oil producer on the Arab side of the Gulf, with production operated by BAHRAIN PETROLEUM CO. (BAPCO), headquartered at al-'AWALI south of the capital, beginning in 1932. The early establishment of an oil industry in al-Bahrayn gave it a head start over its neighbors in modernization. The country nowadays has a large aluminum plant (ALBA) (established in the early 1970s), and an OAPEC-sponsored drydock (established in the mid-1970s). Moreover, al-Muharraq airport is the headquarters of GULF AIR, the principal intra-regional airline in the area, and al-'Awali and 'Isa Town serve as prime examples of modern town planning in Eastern Arabia.

BAIZA (Arabic corruption of pice, a small Indian coin). Different varieties of baizas have been used in Eastern Arabia for nearly a century. The Sultans of OMAN had them minted for use in MUSCAT and DHUFAR and SA'ID BIN TAYMUR had one issue struck for use in the interior. The present Omani baiza was introduced in 1970 along with the RIYAL Sa'idi. The Riyal Sa'idi subsequently became the Riyal Omani, with 1000 baizas equal to one riyal.

BALADIYYAH (plural: baladiyyat). Arabic term for community or municipality. Municipalities were first established in Eastern Arabia in MUSCAT/MATRAH and SHARJAH before World War I and later in al-MANAMAH, al-DAWHAH, ABU DHABI, 'AJMAN, DUBAY, FUJAYRAH, RA'S al-KHAYMAH and UMM al-QAYWAYN. With the reorganization of government in the Sultanate of OMAN after 1970, municipalities were established in over 30 towns of the interior to provide both a nucleus for future self-government and a channel for village improvement and the expression of local grievances.

BALUCHI. An ethnic group comprising a number of tribes in the area known as Baluchistan--the coastal region on the Gulf of OMAN divided between Iran and Pakistan. Baluchis have migrated to the BATINAH Coast of OMAN over several centuries and consequently form a large portion of the population there. More recently, such immigration has increased as Baluchi workers have streamed into Eastern Arabia to satisfy the demand for labor created by the booming oil industries and ancillary enterprises. Baluchis are typically employed as petroleum, port and construction workers or as mercenaries, although many among the more long-term immigrants are farmers and fishermen. One group of Baluchis traveled inland from the Batinah Coast to al-DHAHIRAH province in Oman over a century ago and became an Arabized tribe known as Bani Balush. Most Baluchis are SUNNI Muslims.

BANDAR. Persian word for port. It is included in such place names as Bandar 'Abbas on the Persian side of the Gulf of OMAN, which was ruled by OMAN up to 1868, and Bandar Jissah. The latter port, located about ten miles south of MUSCAT, was granted by Sultan FAYSAL BIN TURKI of Oman to France as a coaling station in 1899 in short-lived defiance of the British position in the Sultanate.

BANI (Arabic plural of <u>ibn</u> [commonly pronounced "bin"], meaning "son"). Bani is frequently used as part of a tribal name. To locate an entry in this dictionary that begins with the word bani, see the proper part of the name (e.g., RIYAM, BANI).

BANYAN [Banian]. Corruption of the Hindu word, <u>baniya</u>, used for the most part by the British to refer to the Indian Hindu merchants who have settled in Eastern Arabia.

BARASTI (plural: barastiyat). The name for a type of dwelling commonly found along the eastern rim of the Arabian Peninsula. Made of date palm fronds and reed mats distributed over a frame constructed from wooden poles.

BARKA. Settlement on the eastern BATINAH Coast in OMAN, about 20 miles from al-SIB on the road leading to NAKHL. Lying offshore Barka are the DAYMANIYAT Islands. Barka was the site of a compact made in 1793 between three sons of AHMAD BIN SA'ID, the founder of the Al Bu SA'ID dynasty. By its terms, Sa'id bin Ahmad was to reside at al-RUSTAQ as the IMAM, Qays bin Ahmad was to receive SUHAR and its territory, and Sultan bin Ahmad was awarded MUSCAT, which he subsequently made the capital of the dynasty.

al-BATINAH. A province of OMAN and the name of the coastal plain that extends for 200 miles along the Gulf of OMAN from the RU'US al-JIBAL mountains in the northwest to the Qurum Hills (near MATRAH) in the east. Most of the Batinah lies in the Sultanate of OMAN although certain northwestern sections belong to various shaykhdoms in the UNITED ARAB EMIRATES (one of the shaykhdoms, al-FUJAYRAH, is situated entirely on the Batinah). Although the plain, which lies between the waters of the Gulf of Oman and the Western HAJAR mountains, varies in width to between 10 and 50 miles, little more than the first mile or less inland from the coast is generally cultivated. This narrow strip is packed with date gardens throughout nearly the entire length of the Batinah. Because of its agricultural and fishing potential, the Batinah is the most densely populated rural area in Eastern Arabia. The inhabitants of the plain are a mixture of Arabs and BALUCHIS (with some Indian traders) and either SUNNI, SHI'I or IBADI in religion. Although the Arab population is generally mixed between GHAFIRI and HINAWI, many villages in the Batinah do not manifest signs of the tribal dichotomy present elsewhere in the Sultanate. Moreover, the Baluchis, unlike their counterparts on the northern side of the Gulf in Iran and Pakistan, as a rule do not form tribal systems in Oman. Prominent Arab tribes are the SHARQIYYIN, QAWASIM, Bani 'Ali, Bani 'UMR, al-HAWASINAH, YAL SA'D, Bani Harras and al-'AWAMIR. The major towns are al-FUJAYRAH, KALBAH, SHINAS, SUHAR, SAHAM, al-KHABURAH, al-SUWAYQ, al-MASNA'AH, BARKA and al-SIB. The area has traditionally supported the Al Bu SA'ID Sultanate.

BAYADIR (singular: bidar). Term used for the Persian or Persianized inhabitants of OMAN who preceded the mass emigration of Arabs to that region. Unlike the BAYASIRAH, the bayadir have largely been assimilated into Arab tribal life, at least in the IBADI area. Nevertheless, their socio-economic function historically has generally been the tending of date gardens for others, for which they are paid in dates.

BAYASIRAH (singular: baysari). The Bayasirah, along with the BAYADIR and the ZATUT, are one of the peoples of Eastern Arabia whose origins have not been definitively traced. They are frequently thought to be the original, pre-Arab inhabitants of the region, as they have never been assimilated into the prevailing Arab social structure. Consequently, their personal status historically lay between an Arab tribesman and a slave. Many Bayasirah communities in al-BAHRAYN and OMAN long ago formed clans that became clients to neighboring Arab tribes.

BAYNUNAH. An area in the western part of the State of ABU DHABI consisting of a stretch of sand dunes with a few brackish wells. Baynunah lies between the GULF coast and the interior region of al-DHAFRAH (of which it is sometimes considered to be a part), and to the east of SABKHAT MATTI. The principal oil terminal of ABU DHABI PETROLEUM CO. at Jabal al-Dhannah is situated within Baynunah.

BAYT (plural: buyut). Arabic word for house. The term is also used in DHUFAR (particularly by the QARA and the AL KATHIR tribes) to denote a clan belonging to a tribe (e.g., the Bayt Ma'ashani of the Qara tribe).

BAYT al-FALAJ. A wadi about 10 miles long located to the immediate south of MUSCAT and MATRAH. The village of RUWI lies at its center. In 1915 tribes from the interior attacked Indian Army troops in this area who were defending the Muscat/Matrah region. After 1970 Bayt al-Falaj became the location of much of the expansion of the Greater Matrah Plan, with apartment buildings, hotels, government ministries, shopping areas and cinemas built between Matrah and Ruwi. The fort located at the northern end of the valley was a summer residence of the Sultans until 1921 when it was converted into the headquarters of the Muscat Levy Corps. In the mid-1970s the fort was still the headquarters of the SULTAN'S ARMED FORCES (SAF). A nearby airstrip was used for both military and commercial flights prior to the construction of a new international airport at al-SIB in 1973.

BAYT al-MAL. An Arabic term with the literal meaning of house of wealth and traditionally applied to the public treasury of the Islamic state. Funds for the treasury were raised primarily from the land tax (kharaj) and a poll tax on non-Muslims (jizyah), and were used to pay salaries, raise armies and improve community property. After the breakup of the Islamic empire into a number of successor states, the term bayt al-mal was also applied to the property of the ruler of the state, which was, however, generally kept separate from the public treasury. With the establishment of more modern institutions, particularly ministries of finance, the use of bayt al-mal has been restricted to a more religious sphere, such as the upkeep of mosques.

BEDOUIN see BADU

BELGRAVE, CHARLES. British 20th-century political adviser to the Government of al-BAHRAYN. Belgrave answered a classified advertisement in The Times (London) in 1926 and began a long career as adviser to Shaykh HAMAD BIN 'ISA AL KHALIFAH, Ruler of Bahrayn (r. 1935-1942). During the period between his recruitment and his retirement in 1957, Belgrave and other British expatriates planted the foundations for a modern administrative apparatus, including the nuclei of present-day ministries and the Bahrayn Police Force. His wife served as Director of Women's Education and his son was Director of Public Relations. Belgrave left a written record of his experiences in al-Bahrayn in his book, Personal Column (London, 1960).

BENT, J. THEODORE. English traveler of the late 19th century. Accompanied by his wife, Mabel, Bent visited al-BAHRAYN, MUSCAT, DHUFAR and the Hadramawt. In Dhufar, they were the first Europeans to travel extensively in the mountain ranges behind Salalah Plain. Their experiences are recounted in their book, Southern Arabia (London, 1900).

BIN see BANI

"BLUE" LINE. The cartographic line established by the Anglo-Ottoman convention of July 29, 1913, which delineated the eastern limits of the Ottoman sanjak (province) of the NAJD, and thus the eastern boundary of the Ottoman Empire in Arabia. The line was drawn on a north-south axis from a point near Zakhuniyyah Island (now part of SAUDI ARABIA) through the Jafurah desert and ending in al-RUB' al-KHALI desert. It definitely established that QATAR was not an Ottoman possession and formed the first tentative boundary in what was to be a long dispute between Saudi Arabia (the successor state to the Ottoman Najd) and the British-protected littoral states of the GULF. In 1935, King 'Abd al-'Aziz of Saudi Arabia presented his counter-boundary, which came to be known as the "RED" LINE.

BOUSTEAD, HUGH. Development Director of the Sultanate of MUSCAT and OMAN (1958-1961) and political agent in ABU DHABI (1961-1965). Boustead's autobiography, The Wind of Morning (London, 1972), recounts his extraordinarily rich life: born in Ceylon, deserting the Royal Navy during World War I to join a South African regiment, fighting in Russia with the White Army, competing in the Olympics, climbing the Himalayas, serving in the Sudan first as Commander of the Sudan Camel Corps and then as a District Commissioner, serving in Ethiopia during World War II and later first British Resident Adviser at Mukalla in the Aden Protectorate. In the late 1960s, Boustead came out of retirement to return to Eastern Arabia where he took up employment in the service of the Ruler of Abu Dhabi at al-'AYN in al-BURAYMI Oasis.

BRITISH BANK OF THE MIDDLE EAST (BBME). The preeminent bank in Eastern Arabia and the GULF. Founded as the Imperial Bank of Persia in 1899, it later established itself in the Arab countries as the Bank of Iran and the Middle East. The bank's interests in Iran were terminated during the Mossadegh era (although new connections were forged later) and it subsequently assumed its present name of BBME. For many years, it was the only bank in the Gulf and at MUSCAT, and so played a quasi-governmental role in fiscal policy and currency affairs until quite recently. The BBME is presently a subsidiary of the Hong Kong Bank Group.

BRITISH INDIA STEAM NAVIGATION COMPANY. The principal steamship line calling at GULF ports during the second half of the 19th and 20th centuries. The company was founded by William Mackinnon and Robert Mackenzie in 1854 as the Calcutta and Burmah Steam Navigation Co. In 1862, the name was changed to British India when the firm received a government mail subsidy following the disbandment of the Indian Navy. For people living in the numerous small ports in the area, "B. I." steamers were for many years their principal contact with the outside--especially Western--world. The line's ownership eventually passed to the Peninsular and Oriental (P and O) Steamship Co.

BU. Local variation of the Arabic word "abu" (plural: aba'), meaning father. It is frequently used in either form as part of a placename or a tribal name (e.g., Abu Dhabi, Bani Bu 'Ali). Entries which include "Bu" will be found under the other component of the name.

al-BURAYMI. Strategic oasis complex in the interior of Eastern Arabia and juncture of the major routes to the GULF (through ABU DHABI Town), the Gulf of OMAN (via al-WADI al-JIZZI) and al-DHAHIRAH province of OMAN. The area has long been a center for caravans. During the 19th century, both SAUDI ARABIA and the Sultanate of OMAN controlled it at different periods. After 1867, the oasis remained in Sultanate hands (with some of the villages passing in the 1890s to the Shaykhdom of Abu Dhabi) until both the Sultanate's and Abu Dhabi's portions were occupied by a Saudi police detachment in 1952. Subsequently the claimants to the oasis agreed to arbitration, which began soon after in Geneva. The tribunal was disbanded, however, after the British member of the tribunal (representing Abu Dhabi and the Sultanate) charged the Saudis with coaching witnesses and bribery. In October 1955, the British-officered TRUCIAL OMAN SCOUTS (TOS) reoccupied the oasis in the name of Abu Dhabi and the Sultanate of Oman, in whose control it has since remained. Saudi Arabia continued to claim its rights to the area until August 1974, when it agreed to recognize Abu Dhabi's claims to sovereignty over six of the villages in the area. The oasis is composed of nine villages. Six of them--al-'AYN, al-Jimi, Hili, Qattarah, al-Mu'tarad and al-Muwayq'i--are inhabited primarily by the DHAWAHIR tribe and, to a lesser extent, by members of the Bani YAS tribe; these villages belong to the state of Abu Dhabi, and are sometimes referred to by the name of the principal village in the group, al-'Ayn. Of the other three (all under the sovereignty of the Sultanate of Oman), al-Buraymi and al-Hamasah are inhabited by the NA'IM tribe, while Sa'arah contains a mixture of Na'im, Bani Jabir, Najadat and Dhawahir. Since the rapid influx of oil money in Abu Dhabi, the Shaykhdom's villages have become manifestly more prosperous than those of the Sultanate, which superimposes a new set of problems atop those of the antecedent political and tribal ones.

BUSHIRE [Bushihr]. Principal port of the Iranian province of Fars. Bushire first gained prominence with the decline of Bandar 'Abbas during the reign of Nadir Shah (1731-1747), and a factory of the (British) East India Co. was established there in 1763. Official British presence dates from 1798, and evolved into the British Consul for Fars and, more importantly, the POLITICAL RESIDENT IN THE PERSIAN GULF, which was responsible for political agents or officers al-KUWAYT, al-BAHRAYN, al-DAWHAH, ABU DHABI, DUBAY, SHARJAH and MUSCAT. Later Iranian objections to the location of the residency on Iranian soil led to its transfer to al-BAHRAYN in the late 1940s.

- C -

CANNING AWARD. The decision in 1861 by which the division of OMAN and ZANZIBAR into separate states was formalized. Under the terms of the will of SA'ID BIN SULTAN AL BU SA'IDI, the Ruler of the expansionist Sultanate of OMAN (r. 1807-1856), his dominions were to be divided between two of his sons, with Majid allotted Zanzibar and Thuwayni receiving Oman. When each of the two attempted to extend his power over the other's territory, the Government of India felt compelled to take a position in the dispute and so appointed the Coghlan Commission to study the issue. At the recommendation of Brigadier M. Coghlan and the Rev. G. P. BADGER, Lord Canning (Viceroy of India, 1858-1862) issued notice to both Majid and Thuwayni that the de facto division of the Sultanate would stand as de jure, with the stipulation that the more wealthy Zanzibar would pay an annual compensation to Oman to equalize the two states' incomes (the ZANZIBAR SUBSIDY). The Award was later agreed to by the French in 1862, and this in effect guaranteed the independence of Oman throughout the 19th and 20th centuries.

COLE, C. S. D. see OMAN

COX, Sir PERCY Z. (1864-1937). British administrator in the GULF during the late 19th and early 20th centuries who was a fine example of the dedicated and skillful civil servants working in the area during that time. Cox's posts included: Political Agent at MUSCAT (1899-1904); POLITICAL RESIDENT IN THE PERSIAN GULF (1904-1913); Secretary in the Foreign Department, Government of India (1913-1914); Chief Political Officer of the Indian Expeditionary Force in Mesopotamia during World War I; acting British Minister to Persia (1918-1920); and High Commissioner for Mesopotamia (1920-1923). Moreover, Cox, through written reports to his superiors, made significant contributions to the advancement of Western knowledge of the Gulf.

- D -

DLF [Dhufar Liberation Front] see DHUFAR REBELLION; POPULAR FRONT FOR THE LIBERATION OF OMAN

DPC see DUBAY PETROLEUM CO.

DALMA ISLAND. A small island off the western coast of the State of ABU DHABI, to which it belongs. At one time, it was a center for the pearl-diving fleets but now is used only as a fishing base. The island is inhabited by several hundred people for whom a school and other modern facilities were built in the late 1960s.

DAMAVAND LINE see DHUFAR REBELLION

al-DAMMAM. A coastal city of eastern SAUDI ARABIA, and the country's main GULF port. Al-Dammam was the site of the Dammam Conference on Eastern Arabian boundaries in early 1952. At this conference an unsuccessful attempt was made to settle the boundaries in dispute between Saudi Arabia and QATAR (which both lie at the base of the Qatar Peninsula and particularly in the KHAWR al-'UDAYD area); and those between Saudi Arabia and ABU DHABI concerning the ownership of al-DHAFRAH region as well as boundaries in the Khawr al-'Udayd. The Saudi delegation was led by then Crown Prince (and later King) Faysal bin 'Abd al-'Aziz Al Sa'ud, while the British Resident in the Persian Gulf, Sir Rupert Hay, represented Qatar and Abu Dhabi. Later in the 1950s, the city became the training location of the OMAN REVOLUTIONARY MOVEMENT (ORM) headed by TALIB BIN 'ALI al-HINA'I who led his army into rebellion against the Sultanate of OMAN in 1957. Talib was finally forced to return in defeat to al-Dammam in 1959 along with most of the other leaders of the revolt.

DANK. Settlement in al-DHAHIRAH province of OMAN at the base of the Jabal al-Abyad Mountain of the Western HAJAR Range, and on the route between 'IBRI and al-BURAYMI oasis. The majority of Dank's inhabitants are from the Al Bu SHAMIS and Bani QITAB tribes.

D'ARCY EXPLORATION CO. see OIL EXPLORATION

DARWISH. An influential merchant family centered in

QATAR but with branches elsewhere in the GULF and the SULTANATE OF OMAN. In Qatar the Darwish family was the first agent for the QATAR PETROLEUM CO. and so acquired an advantage in the competition among firms bidding for contracts related to local development projects. The family is MUHAWWALAH Arab and SHI'I, and thus does not fit in with the dominant tribal groupings of Qatar.

DAS ISLAND. A small island in the GULF located 60 miles offshore ABU DHABI about halfway between Abu Dhabi Town and the QATAR Peninsula. Das was uninhabited prior to 1965, in which year a pipeline was built to it from the nearby Umm al-Shayf oilfield. Subsequently, Das has become the operational center for ABU DHABI MARINE AREAS LTD. (ADMA), the first oil producer in the state. The island now boasts a modern harbor, an airstrip, and a major gas liquefaction plant.

DATE CULTIVATION. The date palm (Phoenix dactylifera) has been a staple element in the life of the Arab from time immemorial. It is as perfectly suited to the needs and culture of Eastern Arabia as the camel. The viability of the area's predominantly OASIS culture is significantly due to the date palm's far-ranging utility: it does not require constant tending (thus allowing cultivators to supplement incomes by nomadism or coastal fishing); it provides necessary shade (supporting a system of three-tiered agriculture, e.g., palms at the top, bananas or oranges in the middle, and alfalfa or grain crops on the bottom); and it can withstand both the drought and excessive salinity that are chronic problems in these areas of aridity and poor soil. The date itself is an important food source for the people of the region. Rich in nutrition (essential in what is otherwise often a poor diet), it can be stored indefinitely and is impervious to contamination. The trunk of the palm is used for construction, the fronds for fuel and mat-making, and the date-stones for camel fodder. Traditionally, dried dates have provided one of the few exports of the area.

al-DAWHAH [Doha]. Capital of the State of QATAR, located on the eastern coast of the Qatar Peninsula. Al-Dawhah was just a small fishing village until oil production began in Qatar in 1949, but by the mid-1970s it had become the largest metropolitan area in the Lower GULF with a population of approximately 135,000. The rapid expansion of al-Dawhah has been preceded by careful planning as is manifested in its modern central square surrounded by a succession of ring roads and suburbs, by its modern international airport and new port facility.

DAYMANIYAT ISLANDS. A group of seven islands lying off the BATINAH Coast (nearest to BARKA). Only two of the islands have names (Jun and Khararabah). None are inhabited and all are simply sandy islets no more than a few feet high.

DAYRAH [Deira]. Urban settlement in the State of DUBAY located on the north side of the estuary (the "Creek") that winds its way through the capital. Dayrah is newer than Dubay Town (located on the south side of the estuary) and was administered by a collateral branch of the Al MAKTUM family until the late 1940s, when it was reunited with Dubay Town. Dayrah's growth as a center for offices and commercial firms was spurred by the establishment of the Dubay Trade School there in 1964, the headquarters of the Trucial States Development Council in 1965, and later by the added attraction of a 60-bed hospital provided by al-KUWAYT.

DEIRA see DAYRAH

DELMON see DILMUN

DE RIBBING, HERBERT see RIBBING, HERBERT DE

al-DHAFRAH [al-Ẓafrah]. The interior region of the western part of the State of ABU DHABI, al-Dhafrah has traditionally been a major grazing area in Eastern Arabia. The region is inhabited primarily by date cultivators and nomadic sections of the Bani YAS and MANASIR tribes. The ruling family of Abu Dhabi, the Al NUHAYYAN (part of the Al Bu FALAH subdivision of the Bani YAS), originated in the LIWA Oasis region of al-Dhafrah, migrating to Abu Dhabi Town two centuries ago.

al-DHAHIRAH [al-Ẓahirah]. One of the western provinces of OMAN, al-Dhahirah is bounded by the HAJAR Mountains on the northeast, the province of Oman on the southeast, the province of Jaw (Jau) and al-BURAYMI on the northwest and the RUB' al-KHALI desert on the southwest. The province's major towns are 'IBRI, Yanqul, Dariz and DANK; its major tribes include al-YA'AQIB, the Bani GHAFIR, al-NA'IM, Bani 'Ali and al-DURU'. Because many of its tribes are SUNNI rather than IBADI, al-Dhahirah generally existed outside the IMAMATE, but as it was rarely administered effectively by the Sultanate of OMAN, it often fell under the influence of SAUDI ARABIA. The inhabitants of al-Dhahirah are mostly date cultivators, camel drivers, and especially in the west, BADU (nomads).

DHAWAHIR [Ẓawahir] (singular: Dhahiri). The largest tribe of al-BURAYMI oasis and probably its original inhabitants. They occupy the villages of al-Jimi, Hili, Qattarah, al-Mu'tarid and al-'AYN, and are divided into approximately a dozen major sections. The tribe has traditionally been at odds with the other major tribe of the oasis, the NA'IM, by whom they were dominated until the Saudi occupation of the oasis in 1800. The Dhawahir were finally brought under the political control of ABU DHABI by Shaykh ZAYID BIN KHALIFAH AL NUHAYYAN in the last decade of the 19th century.

al-DHAYD. An oasis in the Wadi Midfaq near the HAJAR Mountain range, about 30 miles east of the capital of SHARJAH, to which state it belongs. The oasis covers an area of about 15 square miles and is wedged between the mountains and a series of sand dunes. It is only a few miles away from the similar oasis of Falaj al-Mu'alla, which belongs to the state of UMM al-QAYWAYN. Al-Dhayd is a major center of agricultural production in Sharjah, and has received much attention from the state's Ruler, Shaykh SULTAN BIN MUHAMMAD al-QASIMI, who received a degree in agricultural engineering from the University of Cairo.

DHOFAR see DHUFAR

DHOW. The Western word for the wooden sailing craft used for millenia in the Indian Ocean and around the coasts of Arabia. The Arabic word varies according to the type of craft referred to: bum (the largest and, in the past, built mainly in al-KUWAYT); baghalah (another large craft, traditionally built in SUR although much less in evidence nowadays); sambuk (perhaps the most common); and ghanjah.

DHUFAR [Ẓufar; Dhofar]. The southern province of the Sultanate of OMAN, an area of approximately 25,000 square miles with a population of approximately 60,000. Dhufar has three distinct geographical areas: SALALAH Plain facing the Arabian Sea, the mountains (QAMAR,

QARA and SAMHAN ranges) surrounding the Plain and the NAJD, a stony plateau stretching from the mountains to the sandy expanse of the RUB' al-KHALI to the north and the JIDDAT al-HARASIS to the northeast. By virtue of these deserts, Dhufar is practically cut off from the northern part of Oman by land (except for one unpaved track first used by motor vehicles in 1955), and consequently its only accessible neighbor is the eastern region of the People's Democratic Republic of the Yemen (PDRY) to the west. The coastal town of SALALAH is the capital of Dhufar, a part-time residence of the SULTANS, the site of an RAF base, and with an approximate population of 35,000, the largest single settlement in the Sultanate. Moreover, it is in the midst of the greenest area of the country, for the monsoons touch Arabia at Salalah and the mountains behind it. Other towns, all situated on the Plain, include Mirbat, Taqah, Raysut (the site of Dhufar's only harbor, built in the early 1970s), and Rakhyut. The majority of the tribesmen on the Plain and the Najd are of the KATHIR confederation, while the mountains are inhabited almost exclusively by the QARA, Shera, and MAHRA, whose primary languages are related to ancient South Arabia. It is from these tribes that the DHUFAR REBELLION received its greatest support. Principal occupations on the coast are fishing and tending irrigated crops such as wheat, rice and coconuts, while other grains, goats and cattle are raised in the mountains. Dhufar is also one of the few places where the frankincense bush grows, and the ruins of an old South Arabian city near Taqah point to Dhufar's importance in the ancient spice trade.

DHUFAR-CITIES SERVICE. An American oil company to which a concession was granted covering the province of DHUFAR in the Sultanate of OMAN in 1952. The concession had originally been given by PETROLEUM DEVELOPMENT (OMAN) LTD. (PDO) to Wendell Phillips, who turned it over to Cities Service. Exploration wells brought in only water and low grade, non-commercial crude oil. Richfield Oil Company later acquired a 50 per cent working interest, and finally in 1962, Dhufar-Cities Service surrendered the concession to John Mecom-Pure Oil. The latter company's attempts to find oil were frustrated by guerrilla attacks on its trucks and personnel by the incipient Dhufar Liberation Front (DLF). When John Mecom-Pure Oil found no petroleum in commercially viable form, Continental Oil made a brief attempt, but the effort was finally abandoned and the concession reverted back to PDO in 1969.

DHUFAR LIBERATION FRONT see DHUFAR REBELLION; POPULAR FRONT FOR THE LIBERATION OF OMAN

DHUFAR REBELLION. An insurrection against the Sultanate of OMAN. The rebellion began in the early 1960s as a series of sporadic, SAUDI ARABIAN-sponsored attacks against government and oil company property in protest against the petty restrictions placed on the people by Sultan SA'ID BIN TAYMUR who resided in SALALAH, the capital of Dhufar. By 1965, the rebellion had reached the level of a full-scale nationalist movement, led by the Dhufar Liberation Front (DLF). With the attempted assassination of Sultan Sa'id in 1966 by his own Dhufari soldiers, even more restrictions were imposed on the populace, such as placing Salalah off-limits to local tribesmen. This caused increasing numbers of the population to join the rebel forces. By 1968, the movement had heightened its radicalism and was renamed the POPULAR FRONT FOR THE LIBERATION OF THE OCCUPIED ARABIAN GULF (PFLOAG)--its goal the liberation not only of Dhufar or Oman but of all the GULF. Using the People's Democratic Republic of Yemen (PDRY) as a sanctuary, the revolutionaries made many successful forays. Gradually extending their control over all the mountains, capturing several coast towns and raiding others, they even shelled Salalah periodically. The high point of their success was reached in the summer of 1970, when a branch of PFLOAG, the NATIONAL DEMOCRATIC FRONT FOR THE LIBERATION OF OMAN AND THE ARABIAN GULF (NDFLOAG), attacked an army post near IZKI in northern Oman. This raid was the immediate impetus to the coup d'état by which QABUS BIN SA'ID replaced his father, Sultan Sa'id. As a result, a revivified SULTAN'S ARMED FORCES (SAF) stepped up its recruiting campaign and received additional military equipment. Sultan Qabus offered amnesty to all surrendering rebels (which many accepted) and appealed for financial aid in his efforts from his neighbors, particularly Saudi Arabia and ABU DHABI. Moreover, Britain provided officers (both on secondment and on private contract), Jordan loaned army instructors, India dispatched doctors and Iran provided combat troops. By 1972, Salalah Plain was cleared of rebel activity; in 1974 the road through the mountains was kept permanently open; and the Hornbeam Line was built east of, and parallel to, the PDRY border in order to block rebel supply lines; in 1975, the last rebel held town, Rakhyut, was recaptured, and the Iranians built the Damavand Line between the older Hornbeam Line and the PDRY border, thus squeezing guerrilla-controlled territory into an increasingly thin slice of land. This stepped-up military offensive, combined with the Sultan's "hearts and minds" campaign to better the standard of living, had the effect of lessening support for the rebels from their principal backers, PDRY and the People's Republic of China, and put the insurgents in an increasingly defensive posture. Thus, the rebel movement which had been renamed the POPULAR FRONT FOR THE LIBERATION OF OMAN AND THE ARABIAN GULF in 1970 was forced back into more defensible mountain areas. A split arose between the Dhufari and the Gulf elements of the Front in 1974--consequently the "and the Arabian Gulf" was dropped from the name of the revolutionary group, and its remnants began to concentrate on stemming the tide of reverses. A Sultanate offensive begun in October 1975 captured the last rebel-held settlements and resulted in the detention of approximately 130 rebels. On December 11, 1975, Sultan Qabus declared in MUSCAT that the ten-year-old war was officially over.

DIBBA. Port settlement on the Gulf of OMAN at the junction of the BATINAH Coast and the RU'US al-JIBAL. Due to the long confused and highly complex nature of boundary definitions in the area, the sovereignty of Dibba is divided among the Sultanate of OMAN (whose section is normally called al-Bay'ah), the State of al-FUJAYRAH and the State of SHARJAH (whose section is frequently called Husn Dibba). The latter two states belong to the UNITED ARAB EMIRATES. The inhabitants of Dibba are primarily from the SHARQI and QASIMI tribes, although there are some from the SHIHUH tribe. A large battle fought at Dibba during the reign of the Islamic Caliph Abu Bakr (r. 634) brought Oman permanently into the fold of ISLAM.

DICKSON, HAROLD RICHARD PATRICK (1881-1959). Long-time British adviser to the Ruler of al-KUWAYT. H. R. P. Dickson was born in Syria to a British diplomat and breast-fed by a badu (bedouin) girl, a fact which later allowed him increased access to the badu of Arabia. He served in Mesopotamia for the Foreign Office (1917-1919), as Political Agent in al-BAHRAYN (1919-1920), then POLITICAL RESIDENT IN THE PERSIAN GULF (PRPG) and Political Agent in al-Kuwayt until 1936. Subsequently, he was appointed to the post of Chief Local Representative of the Kuwait Oil Co. in al-Kuwayt. Dickson's reputation as an authority on both al-Kuwayt and tribal life in Arabia has been established by his books, The Arab of the Desert (London, 1949) and Kuwayt and Its Neighbours (London, 1956).

DILMUN. Prehistoric city of the GULF. It is now believed that Dilmun was located on al-BAHRAYN island and that there may be a connection between the ancient city and the thousands of tumuli (burial mounds) located south of al-MANAMAH, the capital of the State of al-Bahrayn.

DINAR (plural: dinanir). A traditional unit of currency in Arabia, with the Arabic name being derived from the Roman coin, denarius. The dinar is used in al-BAHRAYN and al-KUWAYT. In both states, one dinar equals 1000 fils. The unit was adopted in these two states in the 1960s, after discontinuation of the use of the Indian rupee.

DIQDAQAH. Rural town in the State of RA'S al-KHAYMAH (a member of the UNITED ARAB EMIRATES), located near the HAJAR Mountains about ten miles south of Ra's al-Khaymah Town. The settlement is the site of the Agricultural Trials Station established in 1955 (the first of its kind in the former TRUCIAL STATES) and an accompanying agricultural school. Because more than two dozen vegetables and fruits are grown at the station, Diqdaqah has become one of the major showpieces of agricultural potential in Eastern Arabia.

DIRAH (plural: diyar). Arabic term for territory generally occupied by, or acknowledged to belong to, a particular tribe. The term normally applies to badu (nomadic) tribes. A badu tribe's dirah, therefore, will usually encompass rights to grazing and water usage within a specified area.

DIRHAM (plural: dirahim). A traditional unit of currency in Arabia, with the Arabic word being derived from the ancient Greek coin, drachma. The dirham is used by the UNITED ARAB EMIRATES (UAE) where one dirham equals 100 fils, and it is a sub-unit of the QATAR

RIYAL which is equal to 100 dirhams.

DIWAN (plural: dawawin). An Arabic word originally referring to the court records of early Islamic administrations. In contemporary Eastern Arabia, it is used to mean the advisory councils which assist the rulers of the GULF states. These diwans typically consist of representatives of various elite groups, such as tribal shaykhs, merchants, religious leaders, members of the ruling family and members of the expatriate communities. In the Sultanate of OMAN, there is a Ministry of Diwan Affairs which acts as a channel of communication between the various interest groups and the Sultan himself. The term diwan should not be confused with MAJLIS, which is a public audience held by the ruler.

DOHA see al-DAWHAH

DOLLAR see MARIA THERESA THALER

DUBAY. The second most important (after ABU DHABI) of the states comprising the UNITED ARAB EMIRATES (UAE). Dubay was a dependency of Abu Dhabi until 1833 when the Al Bu FALASAH section of the Bani YAS tribe established itself there and proclaimed its independence. Occasional violent disputes between the two states lasted up to 1948. The state has an area of approximately 1500 sq. miles and its population in the mid-1970s was approximately 206,000, most of whom live in the capital of the same name. The capital (Dubay Town) lies on the south bank of Dubay Creek opposite the town of DAYRAH on the north bank. Under the leadership of Shaykh RASHID BIN SA'ID AL MAKTUM (the Al MAKTUM form the ruling family), Dubay has developed into the major entrepôt center of the Lower GULF; it has also long been the center for the smuggling of gold, watches and numerous other commodities into India, Pakistan and Iran. The commercial acumen of Dubay's merchants continues to be a major factor in the state's relative prosperity, although oil exports since 1969 have helped to raise the emirate's standard of living and to provide the financial wherewithal that has enabled it to become one of the leading trading centers in the Arab Middle East.

DUBAY PETROLEUM CO. (DPC). Established in 1963 to operate a concession relinquished by Petroleum Development (Trucial Coast) Ltd., a subsidiary of Iraq

Petroleum Co. Originally wholly owned by Continental Oil Co. (Conoco), shares were later acquired by Deutsche Erdöl AG (DEA) and Sun Oil Co. Subsequently, Conoco acquired half-interest in an offshore concession, Dubai Marine Areas Ltd. (DUMA), which had been owned by British Petroleum (BP) and Compagnie Française des Pétroles (CFP). Conoco became the operator for both DPC and DUMA, and DEA and Sun were also brought into DUMA. In 1966, oil was discovered offshore at the Fatah field (some 60 miles from the mainland) and export began in 1969. The difficulty of storing the crude oil prior to offloading was solved by the placement of huge underwater tanks.

DUKHAN. The site of QATAR's major onshore oilfields, situated on the western coast of the Qatar peninsula. The QATAR PETROLEUM CO. began oil production there in 1949, and a pipeline was subsequently laid across the peninsula to the oil tanker terminal at UMM SA'ID. Under the State of Qatar's major economic diversification program, a gas liquefaction plant, an ammonia-urea plant, a flour mill and a cement factory have also been built in the latter area, with the fuel stock for these enterprises being piped across the peninsula from Dukhan.

DURU' (singular: Dara'i). A large nomadic tribe of OMAN whose territory extends from the foothills of al-DHAHIRAH and OMAN provinces to the edge of al-RUB' al-KHALI desert. There are also a few settled Duru' in 'IBRI and on the BATINAH Coast. Most are SUNNI Muslims but some are IBADI: all belong to the GHAFIRI political faction. The loyalty of the tribe's members to the Sultan during the BURAYMI crisis of the 1950s was hesitant; however, they did consistently back the Sultan against the IMAM. Of no less importance, the Duru' also supported the oil company PETROLEUM DEVELOPMENT (OMAN) LTD. when it began operations in their territory in 1954. Since all oil discovered as of 1975 was in Duru' territory, the tribe was receiving substantial cash payments from the company, and was granted priority in the employment of unskilled personnel. According to a decree from Sultan SA'ID BIN TAYMUR AL BU SA'IDI (r. 1932-1970), leadership of the tribe was vested in three shaykhs in a rotating sequence, a most unusual method for Eastern Arabia. Major sub-tribes are the Labat, Najada and Mafafi. The tribe has traditionally been at odds with the Yal

WAHIBAH and closely allied with the YA'AQIB tribe of 'Ibri in the same manner as the JANABAH are with the HIRTH.

DUTCH REFORMED CHURCH see ARABIAN MISSION

- E -

EAST INDIA COMPANY. Originally a trading monopoly chartered in London in 1600, the East India Company eventually evolved into a quasi-government controlling much of India as well as outlying areas in the GULF. The charter was revoked after the Indian mutiny of 1857 and the company was replaced by the Government of India responsible to the India Office in London. At one time, there were actually three East India companies: the other two being the Dutch and French, both of which were supplanted by the British.

ELPHINSTONE INLET see KHAWR al-SHAMM

EMIR see AMIR

EMPTY QUARTER see al-RUB' al-KHALI

- F -

FADL, MUHAMMAD see TOWELL, W. J.

FAHUD. A base camp established by PETROLEUM DEVELOPMENT (OMAN) LTD. (PDO) in 1954, and the site of an oil discovery in 1964. The camp is on the edge of al-RUB' al-KHALI desert in the territory of the DURU' tribe. Fahud is still the center of PDO operations in the interior (other oilfields are at Natih and Yibal). An oil pipeline leads from there through the Wadi SAMA'IL to the coast at Mina' al-Fahal near MUSCAT.

FALAH, AL BU. A subsection of the Bani YAS tribe that migrated from al-DHAFRAH oasis (now part of the State of ABU DHABI) in the mid-18th century and founded the insular Abu Dhabi Town on the east coast of the GULF. The ruling family of Abu Dhabi, the Al NUHAYYAN, belongs to the Al Bu Falah.

FALAJ (plural: aflaj). An Arabic term meaning a water distribution system for agricultural use and used most frequently in OMAN. A falaj consists of a man-made water channel (which may be underground for part of its length and pierced at intervals by vertical shafts). It is generally of communal ownership, each owner of agricultural land buying the right to a certain amount of the total water supplied.

FALASAH, AL BU. A large section of the Bani YAS tribe in the UNITED ARAB EMIRATES. The Al Bu Falasah were part of the Bani Yas inhabitants of ABU DHABI Town until 1833 when a dispute over the succession to the rulership of the shaykhdom caused them to settle in DUBAY to the northeast. An intense rivalry continued between the Al Bu Falasah of Dubay and the Al Bu FALAH of Abu Dhabi, with intermittent wars breaking out up to 1948. The ruling family of Dubay, the Al MAKTUM, belong to the Al Bu Falasah.

FAYSAL BIN TURKI AL BU SA'ID. Sultan of OMAN from 1888 to 1913, he attempted in the 1890s to stem the growing British influence in the Sultanate by a brief flirtation with the French, which was forcibly broken up by the British. A number of significant events occurred during his reign, particularly the build-up and then restriction of the western Asia arms trade (centered on MUSCAT), and the rebellion by interior tribes of the Sultanate following the election of an IBADI IMAM in 1913. In the midst of the revolt, Faysal took ill and passed away; he was replaced by his son, TAYMUR BIN FAYSAL.

FENELON, KEVIN G. A 20th-century British economist and statistician. His first position in the Middle East was as a faculty member at the American University of Beirut. Since 1951, he has served as statistical expert for Iraq, al-KUWAYT, al-BAHRAYN and ABU DHABI, being instrumental in helping to begin statistical offices in each of those states. He has written The United Arab Emirates: An Economic and Social Survey (London, 1973), one of the first books on the modern development of these seven states.

FIRQAH (plural: firaq). Arabic word for team or group. The term is used by the Sultanate of OMAN to refer to the irregular bands of tribal guerrillas of DHUFAR who, having surrendered to the forces of the Sultanate, were thereafter used to protect their tribal territories from their former comrades of the POPULAR FRONT FOR THE LIBERATION OF OMAN (PFLO).

al-FUJAYRAH. One of the seven members of the UNITED ARAB EMIRATES (UAE), al-Fujayrah is the only one to be situated totally on the eastern side of the HAJAR Mountains and not on the GULF. It was part of the State of SHARJAH until 1952 when it was recognized as a separate state by the British. The major tribe is al-SHARQIYYIN from which the ruling family comes. The state has approximately 450 sq. miles and in the mid-1970s had an estimated population of 26,500. Besides al-Fujayrah Town, other settlements (most of which depend on subsistence-level farming and fishing) include Masafi in the Hajar mountains behind the coast and part of DIBBA (to the north of al-Fujayrah Town).

- G -

GENERAL TREATY OF PEACE. The first major treaty between the United Kingdom and the tribal states of the so-called Pirate Coast (southern GULF) signed between January 8 and March 15, 1820. The document was drafted by Capt. T. Perronet Thompson (the interpreter to the British official commanding operations in the area) who had arrived in RA'S al-KHAYMAH in 1819 for that purpose. The treaty's articles outlawed "plunder and piracy on land and sea," mentioned the eventual cessation of the slave trade and required each shaykh to fly a red flag pierced with white. With this treaty, the British assumed the role of arbiter in the affairs of the states of the region, a role that increased in importance with the TREATY OF PERPETUAL MARITIME PEACE (1853), and continued to the official British withdrawal from the region in 1971. With the signing of the 1820 treaty, the area began its transformation from Pirate Coast to TRUCIAL COAST.

al-GHAFAT. A settlement of OMAN province in the Sultanate of Oman located about ten miles from BAHLA at the foot of the Jabal Kawr mountain. It is the headquarters of the Bani HINA, one of the country's most important tribes.

GHAFIR, BANI (singular: Ghafiri). A major tribe in OMAN and the one that gave its name to the GHAFIRI political faction. Today, it is split in two divisions. One lives on the eastern reaches of the JABAL al-AKHDAR near al-RUSTAQ, and has generally supported the Sultan. The other lives around Dariz in al-DHAHIRAH province and is both more badu (nomadic) than the former, and larger; this section tended to support the IMAMATE. Both branches have traditionally feuded with the 'IBRIYYIN tribe.

GHAFIRI-HINAWI. The two major tribal confederations in OMAN. The Hinawi tribes tend to be of YAMANI (also known as Qahtani, or southern Arab) origin and of the IBADI sect of ISLAM in religion while the Ghafiri tribes tend to be of 'ADNANI (also known as Nizari, or northern Arab) origin and of the SUNNI sect of ISLAM in religion. The development of this dichotomy dates from the first half of the 18th century at the time of the civil wars over the succession to the IMAMATE of the YA'ARIBAH dynasty. The two sides coalesced behind the Bani HINA and Bani GHAFIR tribes (thus the names of the confederations). The political nature of the division is underscored by the existence of Hinawi and Ghafiri tribes within each province and frequently in the larger towns, which are traditionally divided into 'ALAYAH (upper) and SIFALAH (lower) quarters. In the last two centuries, the success of tribal rebellions and the periodic revivals of the Ibadi Imamate depended heavily on the extent to which the tribal leader or IMAM could count on support from these factions.

GHALIB BIN 'ALI al-HINA'I. Elected IBADI IMAM of interior OMAN in May 1954 following the death of Imam MUHAMMAD BIN 'ABD ALLAH al-KHALILI. Previous to his election, Ghalib had served as qadi (judge) of al-RUSTAQ and then as assistant to the Imam al-Khalili. After his election, he was dominated by his brother TALIB (the wali, or governor, of al-Rustaq) and the tamimah (paramount shaykh) of the Bani RIYAM tribe, SULAYMAN BIN HIMYAR al-NABHANI. When the Sultanate of OMAN's military forces attacked NIZWA in December 1955, Ghalib resigned as Imam and retired to his home at nearby Bilad Sayt. After Talib returned from exile in SAUDI ARABIA in 1957 with a rebel group (the OMAN REVOLUTIONARY MOVEMENT), Ghalib joined the rebels in Nizwa and then on the JABAL al-AKHDAR. He fled with Talib and Sulayman bin Himyar to Egypt when the Jabal was captured in 1959 and from that time represented himself as the "Imam of Oman" in exile.

al-GHANAM ISLAND. A small island strategically located just off the western tip of Ra's MUSANDAM at the entrance to the GULF. At one time, it was considered as a site for the POLITICAL RESIDENCY IN THE PERSIAN GULF. The island belongs to the Sultanate of OMAN.

GHUBBAT al-GHAZIRAH. Also known as Khawr Habalayn or Malcolm's Inlet, it is one of the two inlets nearly separating the MUSANDAM Peninsula from the RU'US al-JIBAL mountains (the other inlet is KHAWR al-SHAMM; they are separated by the narrow neck of land known as the Maqlab Isthmus). It is wider than the latter inlet and reaches a length of approximately nine miles. The British named it after Sir John Malcolm, 19th-century British ambassador to Persia and later Governor of Bombay.

GOAN. An Indian from the former Portuguese colony of Goa on the eastern coast of India. Many Goans have immigrated to the oil states of Eastern Arabia in search of employment; they typically are engaged as managers and servants in hotels or work as tailors and bank personnel. They are distinctive for their Catholicism in a heavily Muslim milieu.

GOLD. Gold has played an important role in the commercial life of Eastern Arabia, particularly in the State of DUBAY, even though there are no known natural deposits of the mineral anywhere in the area. In 1968, four million ounces, worth over $200 million dollars at the time, were imported by Dubay from London (more than any other country except France and Switzerland). Officially, there is hardly any re-export of that gold but in fact most of it is "smuggled" into India or Pakistan --along with $15.4 million (1968) worth of watches--via motor-equipped DHOWS. But by the mid-1970s, the gold trade had dropped to approximately 15 per cent of what it had been; the decline was so dramatic that banks such as the First National City Bank (New York) and the BRITISH BANK OF THE MIDDLE EAST both stopped dealing in gold. In the years before its oil wealth, al-KUWAYT had also been a center of gold smuggling.

GULF see ARABIAN GULF

GULF AIR. The flag carrier of Eastern Arabia. Formed as Gulf Aviation in the late 1940s as a private company, the British Overseas Airways Corporation (BOAC--now part of British Airways) subsequently became a shareholder in order to keep it solvent. The company is currently owned by the states of al-BAHRAYN, QATAR, the UNITED ARAB EMIRATES and the Sultanate of OMAN, with British Airways as a minority shareholder. The firm has been the object of organized labor strikes at its headquarters in al-Bahrayn, one of the first enterprises in Eastern Arabia forced to contend with such activity.

GWADAR. Port and peninsula on the MAKRAN coast of Pakistan. After Sultan bin Ahmad Al Bu Sa'idi, a contender for the rulership of the Omani SULTANATE, fled from OMAN in 1784, the Ruler of Kalat, Nasir Khan, allowed him to settle in Gwadar. It remained a possession of the Sultans until sold to Pakistan in 1958 for £3,000,000 sterling. Gwadar long provided the Sultanate with most of its BALUCHI soldiers, and in the 20th century, it became a major smuggling port supplying the neighboring hinterland.

- H -

HADR (singular: hadari). Arabic word used to signify someone who lives in a village, town or city. Ordinarily the term is used in contrast to BADU (or in the corrupted form, Bedouin) or nomad. Each regards the other as distinctly inferior, and the tensions between the two groups have been one of the dominant themes of East Arabian and Middle Eastern history since time immemorial.

HAINES, STAFFORD B. Officer of the Indian Navy, who was in charge of surveying the OMAN coast and subsequently the South Arabian coast for the Government of Bombay during the period ca. 1829-1835. His observations of DHUFAR and the KURIA MURIA Islands are among the earliest European writings on the area.

HAJAR. The central mountain range of OMAN, which extends from the MUSANDAM PENINSULA and the RU'US al-JIBAL in the north along a curve almost to RA'S al-HADD in the east. At its center is the JABAL al-AKHDAR massif which rises to more than 10,000 feet; the range is bisected by a number of wadis, the most important of which are al-WADI al-JIZZI, Wadi al-

Hawasinah, WADI SAMA'IL, and Wadi al-'Uday.

The Hajar is divided into two geographical provinces. Western Hajar encompasses the area northwest of Wadi Sama'il, including the towns of NAKHL, al-RUSTAQ, al-'Awabi, and SAYQ; and tribes of Bani KHARUS, part of the Bani RIYAM, part of the Bani GHAFIR, the 'IBRIYYIN, al-HAWASINAH, Bani 'UMR, Bani Kalban and the Bani 'Ali. Southeast of Wadi Sama'il lies Eastern Hajar, with the towns of Sama'il, Bidbid and al-Ghubrah; and its major tribes of Bani Hajir, part of the Bani RUWAHAH, the Rahbiyyin, Siyabiyyin, Bani Wuhayb, al-Masakirah, Bani Battash, al-Hajariyyin and the Bani Jabir. The inhabitants of these areas are date cultivators; they also grow grain crops and raise sheep, goats and cattle.

HAMAD BIN 'ABD ALLAH AL THANI (1893-1946). Designated as heir apparent to his father, Shaykh 'ABD ALLAH BIN QASIM, the Ruler of QATAR from 1913 to 1949. However, Hamad died prior to his father's abdication who was thus succeeded by another son, 'ALI BIN 'ABD ALLAH (r. 1949-1960). Shaykh Hamad's own son, KHALIFAH BIN HAMAD, became Ruler following a bloodless coup d'état of February 1972 in which he ousted Shaykh 'Ali's son (and successor), AHMAD BIN 'ALI (r. 1960-1972).

HAMAD BIN 'ISA AL KHALIFAH. Ruler of al-BAHRAYN from 1935 to 1942. He became Deputy Ruler in 1923 following political troubles and succeeded to the throne on the death of his father, 'Isa bin 'Ali. He signed the concession agreement with BAHRAIN PETROLEUM CO. (BAPCO) and it was during his reign that oil was first discovered, produced and exported. Charles BELGRAVE first came to al-Bahrayn in 1926 as an advisor to Hamad bin 'Isa.

HAMAD BIN MUHAMMAD AL SHARQI. Ruler of the State of al-FUJAYRAH since 1974 and paramount shaykh of the SHARQI tribe. Prior to succeeding his father, MUHAMMAD BIN HAMAD, as Ruler, Shaykh Hamad served as Minister of Agriculture and Fisheries in the Cabinet of the UNITED ARAB EMIRATES.

HAMERTON, ATKINS. A 19th-century officer in the Bombay Army, Hamerton was, in 1840, the first European to visit al-BURAYMI Oasis. His journey, which took him from SHARJAH to al-Buraymi and then through al-WADI al-JIZZI to SUHAR on the BATINAH Coast, was prompted by rumors that the Egyptian commander of troops occupying al-Hasa and the NAJD was contemplating an overland attack on OMAN following the example of earlier Saudi raids.

al-HAMRA'. Settlement of OMAN province located at the base of the JABAL al-AKHDAR mountain, some 20 miles northwest of NIZWA. It is the headquarters of the 'IBRIYYIN tribe.

HANAFI see SHARI'AH

HANBALI see SHARI'AH

HARASIS see JIDDAT al-HARASIS

HARITHI see al-HIRTH

HARRISON, PAUL. An American doctor and missionary, Harrison arrived in OMAN in 1928 and revived the ARABIAN MISSION of the Reformed Church of America, which had been in abeyance since World War I. He was one of the few Westerners allowed to visit the interior of Oman (having attended the illnesses of Imam MUHAMMAD BIN 'ABD ALLAH al-KHALILI on several occasions), and wrote extensively about his experiences.

HASAN, BANI BU (singular: Hasani). A partly settled and partly badu (nomadic) tribe of the JA'LAN province of OMAN whose headquarters is Bilad Bani Bu Hasan. The tribe's members have long been supporters of the Sultan. Largely because they are HINAWI, they have traditionally had the Bani Bu 'ALI as adversaries and the HIRTH, Hajariyyin and Habus as allies.

HAWAR ISLANDS. A group of 16 islands lying close to the western coast of the QATAR Peninsula. The largest, 11 miles in length, is Hawar Island, which contains two small villages; the others are much smaller and are uninhabited. Despite their proximity to Qatar the group has long been claimed by the State of al-BAHRAYN which maintains a small police garrison on Hawar Island.

al-HAWASINAH (singular: Hawsini). An IBADI and HINAWI tribe of the western HAJAR mountain range and BATINAH Coast in OMAN. Although the tribe is not particularly large, it derives considerable influence from its relative cohesion and role as one of the two major suppliers of 'askaris (traditional armed retainers) for the SULTANS. Their headquarters is at al-Ghayzayn in the Wadi al-Hawasinah (which forms part of a route from the Batinah to 'IBRI in al-DHAHIRAH), although others among them have settled around the village of al-KHABURAH on the coast. Their traditional adversaries have been the Bani 'UMR and the Batinah section of the 'AWAMIR.

al-HAZM. A town in the foothills of the Western HAJAR mountain range in OMAN, on the road leading to al-RUSTAQ from the BATINAH Coast. It was the seat of the YA'ARIBAH tribe, which provided the ruling family of Oman from 1625-1737. The great fort that dominates the town was built in the early 18th century under the Ya'rubi IMAM, Sultan bin Sayf.

HENDERSON, EDWARD F. (b. 1917). British diplomat and Arabist, Henderson was educated at Oxford and served in the Arab Legion before coming to the Gulf in 1948 in the service of Petroleum Concessions Ltd. (a subsidiary of the Iraq Petroleum Co.). From then until 1956, he was actively involved in explorations for oil and liaison with Rulers of the states of Eastern Arabia, a role entailing his leadership of the first PETROLEUM DEVELOPMENT (OMAN) LTD. expedition into the interior of OMAN in 1954. He was seconded to the Foreign Service from 1956 to 1959, serving mostly in the TRUCIAL STATES, an area where he had previously (1955) played an important role in decisions which led to the forceful eviction of a Saudi police detachment from al-BURAYMI Oasis ("The Buraymi Oasis Dispute") in ABU DHABI. He subsequently joined the Foreign Service (later, "Diplomatic Service") in 1959 and served as Political Agent in QATAR from 1969 to 1971 when he became the first ambassador to that state, remaining there until 1974. In 1975, he retired from the Foreign Service and went to live in Abu Dhabi.

HINA, BANI (singular: Hina'i). A settled IBADI tribe of OMAN province from which the name of the Hinawi faction of the GHAFIRI-HINAWI dichotomy is derived. The tribe's territory lies north of NIZWA and includes the towns of al-Ghafat (the tribal headquarters), Bilad Sayt and part of Nizwa. The leadership of the "Imamate" revolt in the 1950s was partially supplied by the tribe, as the IMAM elected in 1954 was GHALIB BIN 'ALI al-

HINA'I. Even so, part of the tribe followed its tamimah (paramount shaykh), one of the sons of ZAHIR BIN GHUSN al-HINA'I, who remained loyal to Sultan SA'ID BIN TAYMUR. Because of its loyalty during this troubled period, the tribe was spared the punishment Sultan Sa'id meted out to the Bani Riyam, the other tribe of the revolt.

HINAWI see GHAFIRI-HINAWI

al-HIRTH (singular: Harithi). One of the most important tribes in OMAN, the Hirth are IBADI and HINAWI. The tribe is centered in the Buldan al-Hirth in al-SHARQIYYAH province, which it dominates. The major settlements are al-QABIL (the headquarters), Ibra, al-Mintirib and al-Mudaybi. For the past century the Hirth tamimahs (paramount shaykhs) have been the leaders of the Hinawi faction of tribal politics. SALIH BIN 'ALI was the power behind the IMAMATE of 'AZZAN BIN QAYS (r. 1868-1871) and he instigated the attack on MUSCAT in 1895. His son, 'ISA BIN SALIH, was one of the principal supporters of the Imamate of SALIM BIN RASHID al-KHARUSI (r. 1913-1920) and engineered the election of MUHAMMAD BIN 'ABD ALLAH al-KHALILI as Imam Salim's successor in 1920. He was also the chief negotiator for the Omani tribes in the AGREEMENT OF al-SIB (1920). He was succeeded by his son Muhammad who died a few years later. Muhammad's brother, SALIH BIN 'ISA, then became tamimah, a position he held until forced to flee the country in 1955 following the collapse of the Imamate of GHALIB BIN 'ALI al-HINA'I. Muhammad's son, AHMAD BIN MUHAMMAD, then became tamimah and was entrusted by Sultan SA'ID BIN TAYMUR with control over much of the interior; consequently, he became the most powerful figure in the interior until he was placed under house arrest in Muscat in 1971 because of his criticism of the new regime of Sultan QABUS BIN SA'ID. Qabus was engaged to marry one of Ahmad's daughters before he became Sultan.

Although a small tribe, the Hirth have played a crucial role in Omani politics for much of the past century. The Yal WAHIBAH tribe was long under their leadership. The Hirth have perhaps stronger connections with East Africa than any other Omani tribe. In ZANZIBAR, for example, their kinsmen for many years were influential in the media and commerce and held leading positions in the Arab Association. Consequently, Swahili is a familiar language in al-Sharqiyyah.

HORMUZ, STRAIT OF. The narrow body of water connecting the ARABIAN GULF to the Gulf of OMAN. The northern shore of the approximately 60 mile-wide strait is part of Iran while the southern shore is formed by the MUSANDAM Peninsula, part of the Sultanate of OMAN. As the only waterway leading out of the Gulf, the Strait is of great strategic importance, especially for the many tankers--in the mid-1970s one every 12 minutes--en route to and from the oil terminals in the Gulf area. The Strait became the focus of growing controversy in the 1970s as Iran sought to secure control over its approaches, first by occupation of ABU MUSA and the TUNB ISLANDS, then by proposing a joint ship-checkpoint with Oman, and finally by declaring that a joint Irani-Omani naval force would police the waterway. The name Hormuz also signifies a city located on an island of the same name lying just south of the Iranian mainland. The city of Hormuz was one of the most important entrepôt centers of the area before the Portuguese conquered it in the 16th century. After the Portuguese left, the city was frequently under the control of the Sultanate of Oman, but finally reverted to permanent Iranian ownership in 1868.

HORNBEAM LINE see DHUFAR REBELLION

HURMUZ see HORMUZ

- I -

IPC [Iraq Petroleum Co.] see OIL EXPLORATION

IBADI. The sect of ISLAM to which many of the inhabitants of interior OMAN and the ruling family of the SULTANATE belong. The sect was formed in Basrah (Iraq) in the seventh century as an offshoot of the Khariji sect (founded by the first group of Muslims to break away from the main body of Islam), and its name is derived from one of the founders, 'Abd Allah ibn Ibad. Adherents of the sect in Basrah were soon forced to practice kitman (secrecy) but many were discovered and exiled to the edges of the Islamic empire. Ibadi states were subsequently established in the Maghrib (North Africa), Hadramawt (Southern Arabia) and Oman, but only the latter has survived to the modern era. The survival of Ibadism as the only extant branch of Kharijism is due mainly to its moderation; an important example is its rejection of the traditional Khariji belief that non-Kharijis could be killed for straying from the true path of Islam, i. e. the Khariji interpretation. The religious leader of the Ibadi community is the IMAM, who is chosen by the notables of the community and is then subject to confirmation by the community as a whole. The Ibadi IMAMATE in Oman survived several 'Abbasid conquests of the country; it was finally abolished after the revolt in the interior of Oman in the 1950s. Ibadis do not refer to themselves as such and, generally, their Imam was known as "Imam al-Muslimin" (Imam of the Muslims).

'IBRI. The most important town of al-DHAHIRAH province of OMAN, 'Ibri lies approximately halfway between al-BURAYMI and NIZWA. As a former center for trade in slaves and other commodities, 'Ibri rivalled and was perhaps more important than al-Buraymi. The town's inhabitants are largely from the YA'AQIB and DURU' tribes. It was under the loose control of IMAM MUHAMMAD BIN 'ABD ALLAH al-KHALILI until ca. 1953 when the Imam's wali (governor) was driven out. Its recapture by forces of IMAM GHALIB BIN 'ALI al-HINA'I in 1954 was directly responsible for its subsequent occupation by forces of the Sultanate of OMAN, who acted in concert with the tribes of the area. 'Ibri has been a part of the Sultanate since that time.

'IBRIYYIN ['Abriyyin] (singular: 'Ibri, or 'Abri). A large tribe of OMAN province and the Western HAJAR range with headquarters at al-HAMRA' on the southern slope of the JABAL al-AKHDAR. The tribe's territory extends over the mountain and there are enclaves of Ibriyyin in al-RUSTAQ and al-DHAHIRAH province as well. They were one of the GHAFIRI tribes behind the restitution in 1913 of the IBADI IMAMATE, which they supported until 1955, thereafter aligning with the Sultan against the pro-Imam OMAN REVOLUTIONARY MOVEMENT. The 'Ibriyyin have long been noted for producing mutawwi's (religious leaders) and qadis (judges): Ibrahim bin Sa'id al-'Ibri has been the mufti (chief qadi) of MUSCAT for many years. There is no present connection between the tribe and the town of 'IBRI in al-Dhahirah.

IMAM [and Imamate] (plural: a'immah). An Arabic word

meaning leader, imam originally signified the individual who led the prayers of Islam and only later acquired the meaning of a religious leader who also headed the Islamic state. During the classical IBADI Imamate in Eastern Arabia, the Imam was the religious leader of the community (Imam al-Muslimin) as well as the commander-in-chief of the Ibadi army and the head of state. With the degeneration of the office into dynastic cycles, its religious attributes were overshadowed by its secular functions. The last Ibadi dynasty, the Al Bu SA'ID, eventually dropped all pretensions to the title of imam and ruled as secular leaders only. This opened the way for frequent attempts to re-establish the imam as a religious leader backed by the political power of various tribal shaykhs in the 19th and 20th centuries. Such a quasi-political imamate existed in the interior of OMAN from 1913 to 1955.

INDO-EUROPEAN TELEGRAPH. A department of the Government of India, the Indo-European Telegraph of 1864 was the first to link India directly with London and other centers of Europe. Ardently supported by the Governor of Bombay, Sir Bartle Frere, the telegraph cable went overland to Cape Jask in Persia, then underwater to the MUSANDAM PENINSULA and underwater from there to BUSHIRE, thence overland across Iran and on to Europe. It was suggested at the time that the station on TELEGRAPH ISLAND in the Musandam be combined with a new POLITICAL RESIDENCY IN THE PERSIAN GULF, but this proposal was rejected with good reason (the first three resident station managers died there from the inhospitable climate). The Musandam station was abandoned in 1869 when the cable was rerouted across Hanjam Island in Persia. The telegraph was a great success and used extensively by the Political Resident to keep in touch with his various Political Agents and Officers, and remained a profit-making concern until wireless competition became too great in 1927. By 1931, the Persian section was turned over to the Persian government and the rest was sold to Imperial and International Communications, Ltd. (the name of which was changed to Cable and Wireless in 1934), which subsequently became responsible for communications in the Gulf and other parts of Arabia. The telegraph cable, replaced in 1865 and 1885, was finally abandoned in 1955.

IRAN AND EASTERN ARABIA. Iran's historical relations with its neighbors to the south have existed for millenia, punctuated by periodic invasions and colonization of the Arab side of the GULF, particularly al-BAHRAYN and OMAN. When the PORTUGUESE arrived in the region in the 16th century, they found the Oman coast in the hands of the Kings of HORMUZ; likewise, the present ruling family of al-BAHRAYN captured those islands from Persian-oriented rulers. An invitation from a YA'-RUBI contender for the IMAMATE of Oman paved the way for a Persian invasion of the country in the mid-18th century, which failed--largely because of the efforts of AHMAD BIN SA'ID AL BU SA'ID. By the early 19th century, relations between the two states had improved and a Persian army helped defend Oman from SAUDI attacks in 1815.

More recently, Iranian relations with Eastern Arabia have been complicated by political disputes, in addition to linguistic, ethnic and religious differences (most Iranians are SHI'I Muslims while Eastern Arabia is predominantly SUNNI or IBADI). Although Iran dropped long-standing claims to al-Bahrayn in 1970, its occupation in 1971 of the Gulf islands of ABU MUSA (previously administered by SHARJAH) and the TUNBS (previously administered by RA'S al-KHAYMAH) exacerbated relations with many Arab states. Iran's support of the Sultanate of OMAN in the DHUFAR REBELLION was substantial but received heavy criticism from radical Arab states such as Iraq, Libya and the People's Democratic Republic of the Yemen, which supported the rebels, as well as from traditional Arabian states, suspicious of Iranian intentions towards the Peninsula. For its part, Iran has shown itself adamantly opposed to any government takeover in Eastern Arabia by radical groups, and is concerned about the safety of shipping through the strategic Strait of HORMUZ. It has also resisted the term "ARABIAN GULF" for what it considers to be the "Persian Gulf." Owing to ethnic, national, and geographic considerations--most of the Gulf littoral is under Arab, not Iranian, sovereignty--the latter appellation is opposed by the Arab states. In 1976, the Iranian government briefly recalled its ambassadors from the Arab states in the Gulf in protest to these states' consent to the formation and recognition of a regional press organization called Arabian Gulf News Agency. Another side to the complex relationship is the existence of large Persian, MUHAWWALAH, or Irani-oriented communities on the Arab shore of the Gulf, particularly in al-Bahrayn and DUBAY.

IRAQ PETROLEUM CO. see OIL EXPLORATION

'ISA BIN SALIH al-HARITHI (1874-1946). Tamimah (paramount shaykh) of the HIRTH tribe of al-SHARQIYYAH province in eastern OMAN after the death of his father, SALIH BIN 'ALI, in 1896. 'Isa was also the leader of the HINAWI political faction of tribes and probably the most powerful figure of the Oman interior for the first half of the 20th century. He was one of the principal backers of the IMAMATE of SALIM BIN RASHID al-KHARUSI (r. 1913-1920) and led the attack on MUSCAT in 1915. Upon the death of that Imam, 'Isa worked to secure the election of his choice, MUHAMMAD BIN 'ABD ALLAH al-KHALILI (r. 1920-1954) as his successor. On 'Isa's death in 1946, his position as tamimah of the Hirth fell to his short-lived son, Muhammad, and then to another son, SALIH BIN 'ISA.

'ISA BIN SALMAN AL KHALIFAH. Named heir apparent to the Rulership of al-BAHRAYN in 1958, he succeeded his father, SALMAN BIN HAMAD, in 1961. During his tenure as Ruler, a number of basic reforms in the structure of government have been made, including the establishment of a representative Council of State in January 1970, which helped to pave the way to full independence in August 1971, and the adoption of a constitution in 1973. The first statewide elections ever to be held in al-Bahrayn for a national assembly took place in December 1973. Although the elected deputies were to have served four-year terms, Shaykh 'Isa dissolved the assembly in August 1975, thereby ending prematurely the first experiment of a Lower GULF state in a Western-style parliamentary democracy. 'Isa's son Hamad was named heir apparent in 1965.

ISLAM. The religion of most inhabitants of Eastern Arabia. Islam was founded by the Prophet Muhammad in Mecca (Makkah) and Medina (al-Madinah), two cities of the Hijaz (western Arabia) in the early seventh century. The faith spread rapidly throughout most of the Middle East and North Africa, and extended to parts of Europe and much of Asia as well. The indigenous inhabitants of the Arabian Peninsula are almost entirely Muslim (one who practices Islam), and are predominantly members of the SUNNI sect (the original and orthodox body of Muslims). However, many of the Arabs of Oman are IBADIS (an offshoot of the Kharijis, the first sect to split from the Sunnis). Among the immigrant population in Eastern Arabia (and among the indigenous population of al-BAHRAYN) are many SHI'IS--the second largest sect in size, which is itself divided into several subdivisions, with Iran, Iraq, and the Indian subcontinent accounting for most of the Shi'is--and members of other small Islamic sects. As a religion, Islam is monotheistic and demands comparatively little formal ritual from its followers. The five basic obligations are: (1) the testimony of faith; (2) performance of prayers at five standard times throughout the day; (3) the payment of ZAKAT or alms tax intended for the poor; (4) fasting during the daylight hours of the Islamic month of Ramadan and (5) the hajj, or a pilgrimage to the holy city of Mecca. The traditional interrelationship between religion and state in Islam has been strongly preserved in the Arabian Peninsula, where Islam consequently plays an important role in the politics and society of the states of Eastern Arabia. The basis for legislation and jurisprudence remains the SHARI'AH (or Islamic law), which provides a strong religious basis for the code of individual and family behavior. Within the Sunni interpretation of shari'ah are four schools of jurisprudence: Hanbali, Hanafi, Maliki and Shafi'i. Each of these schools has adherents in Eastern Arabia--an often overlooked factor in the political and historical differences between individual states and various elite groups in the area.

ISLAMIC LAW see SHARI'AH

ISMA'IL BIN KHALIL al-RASASI. A Palestinian long in the service of the Sultanate of OMAN, al-Rasasi was originally recruited by Bertram THOMAS in 1926 as a schoolteacher. When the school was closed, al-Rasasi remained as an adviser to Sultan SA'ID BIN TAYMUR, and over the next 40 years served in various posts, including wali (governor) of MATRAH, inspector of al-BATINAH walis, appeals judge for the MUSCAT civil court, director of education, director of passports and director of the Planning and Development Board. After the coup d'état of 1970, al-Rasasi retired but a year later was named Ambassador to Iran.

ISMA'ILI see SHI'I

IZKI [also, Ziki]. One of the important towns of OMAN province, Izki is situated at the junction of the WADI HALFAYN and the WADI SAMA'IL (called Wadi Bani

Ruwahah at that point) and is the last major settlement on the road heading into the desert towards FAHUD or DHUFAR. Al-SHARQIYYAH province begins just to the south of Izki and the town was an important objective in the 1950s rebellion by the OMAN REVOLUTIONARY MOVEMENT. A guerrilla attack on the army camp outside the town in June 1970 was a catalytic factor in the coup d'état of July 1970 which brought Sultan QABUS BIN SA'ID AL BU SA'IDI to power in Oman. The majority of its inhabitants are from the Bani RUWAHAH and Al Bu SA'ID tribes, with major segments of the town's overall population belonging to the GHAFIRI and HINAWI political factions.

- J -

JABAL (plural: jibal). Arabic word for hill or mountain.

al-JABAL al-AKHDAR. The central massif of the HAJAR mountain range which flanks the BATINAH Coast of OMAN. The Jabal al-Akhdar (its somewhat misleading name is Arabic for Green Mountain) reaches a height of over 10,000 feet and is noted for its large plateau at the 6500-foot level. In this area are a number of villages, including SAYQ, Sharayjah, Minakhir and Wadi Bani Habib, all belonging to the Bani RIYAM tribe. The Jabal is more fertile than most of Oman, marked by a network of mountainside terraces and abundance of grains, apples, peaches, walnuts, pomegranates, wild roses, etc. Its first European visitor was J. R. WELLSTED of the (British) Royal Navy in 1837. Thereafter the Jabal remained inaccessible to Westerners through the 1950s with the exceptions of British Political Agent S. B. MILES and missionary Peter ZWEMER who visited it in 1876 and 1896 respectively. Until conquered by a combination of British troops and units of the SULTAN'S ARMED FORCES in early 1959, it had served as the last refuge for the leaders of the OMAN REVOLUTIONARY MOVEMENT since they were driven from NIZWA in the summer of 1957. A military camp was subsequently established at Sayq and an airfield laid out. In the mid-1970s the plateau was still only accessible by steep footpaths or by air, although there were plans to link it eventually with the plains below by means of a cable car system.

JABAL QAMAR. A mountain range in the Sultanate of OMAN

in the western part of DHUFAR province. The area is inhabited principally by the QARA people and their Shera clients. The range joins the Jabal Qara in the east and marks the western end of the SALALAH Plain. The southern slopes are sheer and come within a mile or less of the Arabian Sea. In the course of the DHUFAR REBELLION, these mountains were the rebels' stronghold and it was only after an Iranian force captured the area's largest town, Rakhyut, and began moving inland in early 1975, that the prospect of their return to the control of the Sultanate of Oman was assured.

JABAL SAMHAN. Mountain range in eastern DHUFAR province of OMAN, which is inhabited principally by the QARA and MAHRA peoples and Al KATHIR tribe. Like the JABAL QAMAR, this range joins to the Jabal Qara and marks the eastern end of the SALALAH Plain. The area is noted for its frankincense trees, which is the probable explanation for the location of an ancient South Arabian city at Khawr Rawri on the nearby coast. Although during the late 1960s and early 1970s much of the Jabal Samhan was held by guerrillas participating in the DHUFAR REBELLION, it was the first of Dhufar's three mountain ranges to be cleared of rebel operations.

JABRIN see BAHLA

JA'LAN. The easternmost geographical province of OMAN; bounded on the east by the remnants of the HAJAR mountain range, on the south by the Arabian Sea, on the west by the WAHIBAH SANDS and on the north by al-SHARQIYYAH province. The internal politics of the province have long been dominated by the rivalry of the Bani Bu 'ALI and Bani Bu HASAN tribes, although the Bani Hishm, Yal WAHIBAH and al-Masharifah tribes also inhabit the area. Major towns are Bilad Bani Bu 'Ali, Bilad Bani Bu Hasan, al-Kamil and SUR (although the last-named is technically not a part of the province, being on the Gulf of OMAN coast). The area has long been considered xenophobic and rarely was controlled by the Sultanate of OMAN: various shaykhs of the Bani Bu 'Ali have on occasion claimed to be the ruler (AMIR) of Ja'lan.

JANABAH (singular: Junaybi). One of the three great nomadic or badu tribes of OMAN, the Janabah territory stretches from NIZWA in the north to the Arabian Sea, and along the coast from DHUFAR in the west to the

Gulf of Masirah in the east. Much of this territory they dispute with the Yal WAHIBAH. Large segments of the tribe, however, are sedentary and are fishermen and sailors of SUR and MASIRAH Island; they also own date palms in 'Izz, 'Afar and ADAM. It is largely because their territory covers such a large area that the tribe is politically fragmented. In the last several decades, the Janabah have lost position to both the DURU' (because of oil finds in the latter's territory) and the Yal Wahibah (who benefited from their relationship with the HIRTH). To counteract this regression, the Janabah entered into a close relationship with the Bani RIYAM in order to benefit from an association with the GHAFIRI leader, SULAYMAN BIN HIMYAR al-NABHANI. But this relationship foundered when the OMAN REVOLUTIONARY MOVEMENT, which Sulayman supported, failed and he fled the country in 1959. The Janabah are SUNNI and belong to the Ghafiri faction.

JAWASIM [Jasimi] see QAWASIM

JEBEL see JABAL

JIDDAT al-HARASIS. A stony desert lying between DHUFAR and geographical OMAN and inhabited exclusively by the Harasis (singular: Harsusi) tribe. This small tribe is of uncertain origin and speaks its own language in addition to Arabic. There is speculation that the Harasis are a remnant of the ancient nations that occupied DHUFAR and southern Arabia (as are the QARA and the MAHRA), although a number of neighboring Arab tribesmen seem to have assimilated with the Harasis.

JILUWI, BIN see SA'UD BIN JILUWI

JIMENEZ REPORT see RIBBING, HERBERT DE

JUFAYR. BAHRAYNI port on the southern side of the city of al-MANAMAH. The site was acquired for use as a British naval base in 1935 and was taken over by the U. S. Navy as headquarters for its Middle East Force (consisting of a destroyer and two tenders) after the British military withdrawal in 1971. During the October 1973 Arab-Israeli War, the Bahrayn Government demanded the eventual American evacuation of the base but this ultimatum was later rescinded. In November 1975 in a move designed to lessen the grounds for possible criticism of al-Bahrayn in intra-Arab councils, the government announced that the U. S. would have to evacuate the facilities at Jufayr by mid-1977.

JULFAR. A port on the southeastern coast of the GULF. For centuries the QAWASIM, one of the most important tribes in Eastern Arabia, put to sea from Julfar, frequently menacing ships until the British captured the port and destroyed it in 1819. Today it is known as RA'S al-KHAYMAH and serves as the capital and principal town of the state of the same name.

JUNAYBI see JANABAH

- K -

KA'B, BANI (singular: Ka'bi). An OMANI tribe with both settled and badu (nomadic) sections. The badu are centered around al-BURAYMI. Their allegiance to the Sultanate of OMAN was in question during the SAUDI ARABIAN attempt of the 1950s to annex al-Buraymi. The settled sections are in the vicinity of Mahadah at the entrance to the WADI al-JIZZI and also between SUHAR and LIWA on the BATINAH Coast. The members of the tribe are SUNNI (and HANBALI in particular) in religion and belong to the GHAFIRI political faction. They are allied to the Bani QITAB.

KALBAH. A town in the UNITED ARAB EMIRATES (UAE) located on the Gulf of OMAN, immediately south of al-FUJAYRAH. Although presently part of the state of SHARJAH (one of the seven member states of the UAE), Kalbah itself was an independent state from 1936 to 1952.

KATHIR, AL (singular: Kathiri). One of the most widespread tribes of Eastern Arabia. Its origins are in the Hadramawt, formerly part of the Aden Protectorate (now the People's Democratic Republic of the Yemen), which included a Kathiri State in treaty relationship with the British until 1967. The members of the tribe in Eastern Arabia are distributed from OMAN province to the BATINAH COAST, but the majority are located in the southern province of DHUFAR. Three large subdivisions (called bayt) are located on SALALAH Plain--the Rawwas; the Shanafir (singular: Shanfari); and the Marhun--while another large grouping (Bayt Kathir) occupies the NAJD between the mountains and al-RUB' al-

KHALI desert. Although they are SUNNI and HINAWI, the Dhufar branches are too far away to take part in the tribal and genealogical politics that have traditionally formed such an important part of the social fabric in many other areas of the Sultanate. They arrived in Dhufar later than the South Arabian tribes of the mountains and today dominate trade. The Bayt Kathir were the original instigators of the DHUFAR REBELLION, although they seem to have lost influence quite early.

al-KHABURAH. After SUHAR, the second largest town of the BATINAH Coast. The inhabitants are mainly members of the Bani 'UMR and HAWASINAH tribes, a large number of BALUCHIS and a small KHOJA community. The town is also a gateway to one of the principal passes through the Western HAJAR Mountains, via the Wadi al-Hawasinah to 'IBRI.

KHALID BIN MUHAMMAD al-QASIMI. Ruler of the State of SHARJAH from 1965 to 1972. He came to the rulership in 1965 after a coup d'état ousting Shaykh SAQR BIN SULTAN, which was maneuvered with British assistance. Although of great moral integrity, he suffered from a lack of administrative decisiveness. In addition, he became unpopular as a result of the inferior political position accorded Sharjah vis-à-vis ABU DHABI and DUBAY when the UNITED ARAB EMIRATES was established in 1971. Moreover, Khalid suffered much criticism for the Iranian occupation of ABU MUSA Island in November of the same year, and, in particular, for his having concluded an agreement with the Shah of Iran that permitted the permanent garrisoning of Iranian military forces on the island. He was assassinated during an unsuccessful attempt by Shaykh Saqr bin Sultan to regain the rulership in January 1972.

KHALIFAH, AL. The ruling family of the State of al-BAHRAYN. Part of the Bani 'UTUB tribe of central Arabia, the Al Khalifah migrated from al-KUWAYT in the mid-18th century to al-ZUBARAH on the western coast of the QATAR Peninsula. In 1783, they captured (with the aid of the Kuwayti branch of the 'Utub) the archipelago of al-Bahrayn from its Persian sovereigns and some years later made al-MANAMAH their capital. Recent Al Khalifah Rulers of al-Bahrayn have been HAMAD BIN 'ISA (r. 1935-1942), SALMAN BIN HAMAD (r. 1942-1961) and 'ISA BIN SALMAN (r. 1961-).

KHALIFAH BIN HAMAD AL THANI. Succeeded his cousin, Shaykh AHMAD BIN 'ALI, as Ruler of QATAR in February 1972. Previously Khalifah had served as Director of Police and Internal Security, Director of Education, Minister of Finance and Petroleum Affairs, Prime Minister, and Deputy Ruler. Upon his succession in 1972, he established the State Advisory Council as required by the Temporary Constitution of 1970 (his predecessor Ahmad bin 'Ali's refusal to establish it had contributed to his downfall). Moreover, in a reform of the scandalous practices of various members of the Al Thani ruling family, Khalifah abolished the practice of allocating a quarter of the State's oil revenues to the personal account of the Ruler. Khalifah rose to the Rulership by organizing a coup d'état against Ahmad in February 1972 as he and his numerous supporters feared that Ahmad's son, 'Abd al-'Aziz bin Ahmad, would be made Ruler in his place.

KHALILI, AWLAD. An OMANI tribal clan based in WADI SAMA'IL. Originally from the Bani KHARUS tribe, they have provided the tamimah (paramount shaykh) of the Bani RUWAHAH tribe for several generations. The Khalilis first came into prominence when SA'ID BIN KHALFAN al-KHALILI served as one of the principal backers of Imam 'AZZAN BIN QAYS, who held MUSCAT from 1868-1871 with Sa'id as his wazir (minister or adviser). Sa'id's grandson, MUHAMMAD BIN 'ABD ALLAH, served as IBADI IMAM at NIZWA from 1920 to 1954, and two of Muhammad's nephews held high posts in the government of Sultan QABUS BIN SA'ID AL BU SA'ID (1970-).

KHANJAR. A dagger carried in a silver sheaf with a distinctive 45° angle. The khanjar is carried by nearly all the tribesmen of OMAN. In the mid-1970s, its function was not so much for defense as for status. Similar daggers elsewhere in Arabia are known as jambiyah.

KHARUS, BANI (singular: Kharusi). A medium-sized OMANI tribe of the western HAJAR mountain range, residing mainly in the Wadi Bani Kharus on the seaward side of the mountains and in the villages of al-'Awabi (their headquarters), al-RUSTAQ and NAKHL. They are IBADI and GHAFIRI, and have a close, almost "client" relationship with the Bani RIYAM. The tribe supplied a dynasty of medieval Ibadi IMAMS, their last representative in that post being SALIM BIN RASHID al-KHARUSI, who was Imam from 1913 to 1920. Two of his sons, Yahya and 'Abd Allah, subsequently served as walis for Imam MUHAMMAD BIN 'ABD ALLAH al-KHALILI but the Bani Kharus apparently did not support his successor, GHALIB BIN 'ALI al-HINA'I.

KHASAB. The major settlement and port of the RU'US al-JIBAL area at the extreme eastern end of the Gulf. Khasab's origins are prehistoric and a Portuguese fort was built there in the mid-17th century. It is under the sovereignty of the Sultanate of OMAN and is one of three villages in the area where a wali (governor) resides, the other two being DIBBA and Bukha. The indigenous inhabitants of Khasab are almost exclusively from the SHIHUH tribe.

KHATIR see RAFIQ

KHATM MILAHAH. A settlement at the western end of the Sultanate of OMAN'S portion of the BATINAH Coast. It marks the border between the Sultanate and the UNITED ARAB EMIRATES (specifically, the state of al-FUJAYRAH).

KHAWR. A Persian word used for a saltwater inlet and frequently included in the place names of such inlets in Eastern Arabia.

KHAWR FAKKAN. The principal port and town on the Gulf of OMAN at the junction of the BATINAH Coast and the RU'US al-JIBAL Mountains. A noted center of trade and sailing fleets for centuries, Khawr Fakkan was a prosperous town prior to being destroyed by the PORTUGUESE admiral, Affonso d'Albuquerque, in 1506. It was rebuilt as one of the forts and centers of the fleet of the QASIMI tribe until once again destroyed by a combined force mounted by the British and the Sultanate of OMAN in the early 19th century. Today, it is the second largest settlement in the State of SHARJAH.

KHAWR HABALAYN see GHUBBAT al-GHAZIRAH

KHAWR al-SHAMM. Also known as Elphinstone Inlet, it is one of the inlets nearly separating the MUSANDAM PENINSULA from the RU'US al-JIBAL mountains (the other inlet is GHUBBAT al-GHAZIRAH; they are separated by a narrow neck of land known as the Maqlab Isthmus). The Khawr was used for centuries by QASIMI pirates who would wait there in hiding for passing ships. When the British began their efforts to end piracy in the Gulf, the Qasimi ships often eluded capture by disappearing into the Khawr al-Shamm. European knowledge of the inlet dates from the British survey of 1820, which revealed the existence of a nine-mile long sunken canyon. Nearly half a century later, a British outpost was established on TELEGRAPH ISLAND in the Khawr. The British named it after Mountstuart Elphinstone, early 19th-century Governor of Bombay.

KHAWR al-'UDAYD. A marshy inlet at the eastern base of the QATAR Peninsula. The Qubaysat section of the Bani YAS tribe made several unsuccessful attempts in the 19th and early 20th centuries to secede from ABU DHABI and settle at Khawr al-'Udayd. Sovereignty over the area was claimed first by the States of Qatar and Abu Dhabi and then by SAUDI ARABIA, which included the Khawr in its 1949 claim to much of Abu Dhabi. The boundary problem between Saudi Arabia and Abu Dhabi was settled in August 1974. At that time Abu Dhabi, which claims sovereignty in the area, agreed to grant Saudi Arabia special access rights. For some years there have been reports that a port will eventually be built in the vicinity to facilitate the export of oil from the RUB' al-KHALI region of Saudi Arabia. The onshore boundary line between Abu Dhabi and Qatar in this area had not been officially demarcated by the mid-1970s. However, the governments of both states were believed to acknowledge shared sovereignty over it, with the de facto border being a line extended coastward from their offshore boundary, delineated in 1969.

KHOJA. An originally Indian Islamic group that has founded communities along the coast of OMAN. Generally known to the Arabs as liwatiyah (singular: lutiyah), the Khojas have occupied the Sur al-Liwatiyah (Khoja Quarter) in MATRAH for several centuries. Other communities of Khojas exist in BARKA, SUHAR, al-KHABURAH and al-MASNA'AH on the BATINAH Coast. They were originally Isma'ilis (a subgroup of the SHI'I sect of Islam), but virtually all those remaining in Oman have become Ithna'ashari Shi'is (the main group of Shi'is). They are merchants and silversmiths and have long dominated the Matrah suq (market). They do not participate in tribal politics and have invariably supported the SUL-

TANS. Nevertheless, they are generally excluded from important government positions in the Sultanate.

KHOR see KHAWR

KHURAYBAN, AL BU. Principal section of the NA'IM tribe of Peninsular OMAN. They occupy the villages of al-Buraymi and Sa'arah in al-BURAYMI oasis, Hafit and DANK in the DHAHIRAH province of the Sultanate of OMAN, and 'AJMAN on the Gulf coast. The ruling family of the State of 'Ajman is of the Al Bu Khurayban, as is the tamimah (paramount shaykh) for the Na'im as a whole (including the Al Bu SHAMIS section). The Al Bu Khurayban established a close relationship with the SAUDI garrison that occupied al-Buraymi oasis from 1952 to 1955. They are SUNNI and, more particularly, HANBALI, having become MUWAHHIDUN or Wahhabis in the early 19th century, and GHAFIRI.

KURIA MURIA ISLANDS. A group of five islands in the Arabian Sea off the southern coast of the Sultanate of OMAN, of which only the largest (Hallaniyah) is inhabited. They were given by Sultan SA'ID BIN SULTAN (r. 1807-1856) to Queen Victoria of England in 1854 and were returned to Oman in 1967. As they had been administered until that time from the (British) Colony of Aden, the People's Republic of Southern Yemen (later People's Democratic Republic of the Yemen) claimed them on independence and even appointed a governor for them. At one time the islands were exploited for their guano deposits.

al-KUWAYT AND EASTERN ARABIA. Al-Kuwayt was one of the first states (the other was al-BAHRAYN) to amass sufficient oil revenue to begin a radical transformation of its economic and social base. Subsequently, the states of Eastern Arabia benefitted greatly from al-Kuwayt's generous donation of hospitals, clinics, government buildings, schools, and subsidies to help pay the cost of the personnel required to administer many of these facilities. Moreover, both al-Kuwayt's system of state welfare services and its generous foreign aid program served as examples to these states when some of them--in particular QATAR and ABU DHABI--began to acquire substantial oil revenues of their own.

Al-Kuwayt has at times unwittingly been linked to unrest in some of the other states in the region. This unrest has commonly been channeled via Gulf students or laborers who, during their time of study or work in al-Kuwayt, have come into contact with such organizations as the ARAB NATIONALISTS MOVEMENT and later the POPULAR FRONT FOR THE LIBERATION OF OMAN (PFLO).

- L -

al-LIWA. The 30-40 villages of al-Liwa, also known as al-Jiwa, comprise one of the largest and most important oasis complexes in Eastern Arabia. Located in the western portion of the State of ABU DHABI, the area is shared mainly by the Bani YAS and MANASIR tribes. It is the ancestral home of the Al NUHAYYAN, the ruling family of Abu Dhabi. Al-Liwa is also the name of a town on the BATINAH Coast in the Sultanate of OMAN.

LIWATIYAH see KHOJA

LORIMER, JOHN G. A 19th- and 20th-century official of the Government of India, Lorimer served in the Foreign Department and also as POLITICAL RESIDENT IN THE PERSIAN GULF. He is remembered as being the principal compiler and editor of the Government of India's monumental <u>Gazetteer of the Persian Gulf, 'Oman and Central Arabia</u>. This work, based on reports of officials stationed in the area, contemporary writings and original research, is in two parts, historical and geographical, and is easily the most comprehensive reference work on the area as it existed up to the end of the 19th century.

LUCE, SIR WILLIAM H. T. (b. 1907). British diplomat. He was educated at Cambridge and served in the Sudan Political Service for over two decades until 1956. At that time, he was named Governor and Commander-in-Chief of Aden Colony, a post in which he served for four years. Following that Governorship, he served as POLITICAL RESIDENT IN THE PERSIAN GULF from 1961 to 1965. After the British government's decision to terminate its special treaty relationship with the Gulf states, Luce was appointed Personal Representative of the Foreign and Commonwealth Secretary for Persian Gulf Affairs (1970-1972) with the responsibility of ensuring an orderly transition to independence. He has also served as a director of a number of firms prominent in the area, such as Eastern Bank, Chartered Bank and Gray Mackenzie.

- M -

McKIRDY, ARCHIBALD see TOWELL, W. J.

MAHRA (singular: Mahri). One of several peoples with a non-Arabic language as their primary tongue who inhabit DHUFAR and Southern Arabia (the others being the QARA, the Shehra, the Batahirah and, according to some accounts, the original Harasis). They are generally thought to have migrated into their present territory approximately 1000 years ago along with the Qara (i. e., after the original Shehra inhabitants but before the Al KATHIR). Although a number of Mahra inhabit the JABAL SAMHAN mountain range in eastern Dhufar, the majority are in the eastern or Mahra area of the People's Democratic Republic of the YEMEN (PDRY), where they inhabit the Sixth Governorate. Due to their ethnic and loose linguistic relationship to the Qara, who were in rebellion against the government of the Sultanate of OMAN from the early 1960s to the mid-1970s, it was often thought that much local support for the DHUFAR REBELLION existed in PDRY's Sixth Governorate (in addition to the official support that PDRY gave the rebels).

MAJLIS (plural: majalis). An informal meeting and consulting session that anyone, citizen or foreigner, may attend in order to confront the Ruler of a state directly with local or personal problems he believes the Ruler can solve. Through the majlis, personal contact is theoretically, and in many instances actually, maintained between the Ruler and all levels of society. The institution of the majlis is testimony that a degree of democracy exists within the traditional social norms of the communities of Eastern Arabia.

MAKRAN. The region along the northern coast of the Gulf of OMAN that comprises the southern part of Baluchistan, divided between Iran and Pakistan. It includes the port of GWADAR, a former possession of the Sultanate of OMAN, which has long provided Baluchis for the Omani military. Since the discovery of oil in many of the states of Eastern Arabia, many more Baluchis have migrated to these states in search of short-term jobs.

MAKTUM, AL. The ruling family of the State of DUBAY, belonging to the Al Bu FALASAH section of the Bani YAS tribe. The Al Bu Falasah seceded from ABU DHABI in 1833 and settled at Dubay under the leadership of Maktum bin Buti Al Maktum. Through the next century-and-a-half, the family pursued rivalries with the ruling families of the neighboring states--the QAWASIM of SHARJAH to the north and the Al NUHAYYAN of Abu Dhabi to the south. After the formation of the UNITED ARAB EMIRATES (UAE) in 1971, members of the family assumed many posts in the federal government, including the Vice Presidency, the Premiership and several key ministerships. The most recent member of this family to serve as Ruler of Dubay is Shaykh RASHID BIN SA'ID (r. 1958-).

MALCOLM'S INLET see GHUBBAT al-GHAZIRAH

MALIKI see SHARI'AH

al-MANAMAH. The capital and main city of the State of al-BAHRAYN, located on the northern tip of al-Bahrayn Island. A city of approximately 100,000 inhabitants in the mid-1970s, it is the center of an intensely cultivated region of date palms and citrus trees. It is one of the most developed cities in the Gulf and has an extremely heterogeneous population. The Western presence is pronounced, with a mission and hospital of the ARABIAN MISSION of the Reformed Church of America, a Catholic mission, and a small U.S. naval base in JUFAYR harbor. From the late 1940s to 1971, it was the headquarters of the POLITICAL RESIDENCY IN THE PERSIAN GULF (PRPG), through which British policy in the area was administered. The city is connected by a causeway to the island of al-MUHARRAQ to the north, the second-largest city of the state and the site of an international airport. The name al-Manamah also applies to an oasis in 'AJMAN.

MANASIR (singular: Mansuri). One of the most widespread tribes of Eastern Arabia. The Manasir are almost exclusively badu (nomadic) and range from al-BURAYMI oasis in the east to QATAR and al-Hasa (in SAUDI ARABIA) in the west. A few settled members reside in SHARJAH and RA'S al-KHAYMAH. They are concentrated in al-DHAFRAH and al-LIWA oases in western ABU DHABI, which they share with the Bani YAS tribe. They have been allied with the latter tribe since the early 19th century and have largely supported the Bani Yas rulers of Abu Dhabi in the latters' disputes with the QASIMI tribe and Saudi Arabia. The Manasir are SUNNI (and Maliki in matters of Islamic law) and HINAWI; their major sections are the Al Bu Mundhir, the Al Bu Rahmah and the Al Bu Sha'ar.

MAQLAB ISTHMUS see MUSANDAM PENINSULA

MARIA THERESA THALER (Dollar). A large silver coin (ca. 1 1/2" in diameter) often called a RIYAL (after the Spanish real de plata). Once universally used throughout Arabia, it survived as a currency in Yemen and OMAN until quite recently. The original thalers were of Spanish, Dutch, German and Austrian origin but few are in existence today. Most thalers found nowadays are copies of the Austrian thaler (Maria Theresa was Empress of Austria) minted mainly in Great Britain and Germany; regardless of their origin these thalers bear the date of 1780.

MARITIME PEACE, TREATY OF PERPETUAL. The culmination in 1853 of a series of truces arranged to prevent warfare between the numerous states of the Lower Gulf, which had long disrupted maritime trade and pearling. The first of these truces was arranged in 1835 and several others followed until a Ten-Years' Truce was signed in 1843. Finally, the five ruling shaykhs of the area (i.e., the rulers of ABU DHABI, DUBAY, 'AJMAN, SHARJAH and RA'S al-KHAYMAH, and UMM al-QAYWAYN) met with Col. A. B. Kemball, the POLITICAL RESIDENT IN THE PERSIAN GULF, in early May of 1853 and agreed that they and their heirs and successors would abide by a total maritime truce in perpetuity. Thereafter, the area encompassing these states became known as the TRUCIAL COAST.

al-MASIRAH. An Arabian Sea island that is approximately 40 miles long and lies off the southeastern coast of OMAN adjacent to the Gulf of al-Masirah. The island is inhabited by a small number of fishermen from the JANABAH tribe. It is also the site of one of the two (British) Royal Air Force (RAF) bases in Oman (the other being in SALALAH) and is used both as a staging and refueling post on the way to the Far East (originally having performed this role as part of the old South Arabian Air Route) and as a major communications facility.

al-MASNA'AH. One of the larger villages along the BATINAH Coast of OMAN, located midway between al-SUWAYQ and BARKA. The settlement is at the coastal end of the wadi (watercourse) and road leading to al-HAZM and al-RUSTAQ in the Western HAJAR Mountains. Nearby is Ra's Suwadi, a small cape and island, the only deviation from the sandy beaches found along the entire length of the Batinah. The inhabitants are mainly BALUCHI and Arabs from the YAL SA'D tribe, plus a few KHOJAS. When al-Masna'ah was captured in 1874 by Ibrahim bin Qays Al Bu SA'ID (the brother of Imam 'AZZAN BIN QAYS) and the Yal SA'D tribe, the British were forced to bombard the fort in order to dislodge them and thereby protect the village's Indian merchants.

MASQAT see MUSCAT

MATRAH. Commercial center of the Sultanate of OMAN and one of its major towns, located on the coast about five miles northwest of MUSCAT. Its commercial role has been facilitated by its fine natural harbor, where Mina' Qabus (Port Qabus) was built in the early 1970s, and its position as a gateway to the interior. Traditionally, the town was protected by an old Portuguese fort (built in the mid-16th century) and a score of watchtowers sited on the surrounding peaks. The population is particularly heterogeneous, including sizeable communities of Arabs, BALUCHIS, KHOJAS, Hindus and Africans. It has been the site of a hospital run by the ARABIAN MISSION of the Reformed Church of America since the turn of the century. Since the accession of Sultan QABUS BIN SA'ID in 1970, Matrah has prospered with a new port, offices and shops, corniche and divided highway linking the old town with the Wadi BAYT al-FALAJ, site of the Greater Matrah Plan.

MIDWAY see THAMARIT

MILES, SAMUEL BARRETT (1838-1914). Officer of the Indian Army and representative of the Government of India at several places in Eastern Arabia, notably MUSCAT. Miles served at Muscat from 1872-1886 (although he was frequently called away to serve at other posts). He also served in Aden, Baghdad, ZANZIBAR and India. After leaving Muscat in 1886, he was made acting POLITICAL RESIDENT IN THE PER-

SIAN GULF until recalled a year later to India. He retired in 1893. During his period as Political Agent at Muscat, he traversed practically the entire interior of OMAN, being the first Westerner to do so in 30 years, and came to know it better than any other Westerner until the late 1950s. He was one of only two Westerners to reach the JABAL al-AKHDAR between 1837 and 1959 (the other being missionary Peter ZWEMER). After his retirement, he combined his personal knowledge of the country with his studies of the classical authors and continued a tradition of Government of India officials by adding to the store of knowledge of the area (in the line of the Rev. G. P. BADGER and E. C. ROSS). A substantial portion of this research was collected and published in The Countries and Tribes of the Persian Gulf (London, 1919).

MINA' (plural: miwan or miyan). Arabic word for port. Among the new ports of the area bearing this prefix are: Mina' Salman (al-MANAMAH), Mina' Rashid (DUBAY); Mina' Qabus (MATRAH), and Mina' al-Fahal, site of the PETROLEUM DEVELOPMENT (OMAN) LTD. complex immediately west of MATRAH.

MUHAMMAD BIN 'ABD ALLAH al-KHALILI (d. 1954). Elected as IBADI IMAM of OMAN in 1920 after the assassination of Imam SALIM BIN RASHID al-KHARUSI. He was elected as a protégé of 'ISA BIN SALIH al-HARITHI (who was reported to be his son-in-law), although he later became a much respected political, as well as religious, figure of the interior in his own right. With his death a vacuum ensued in the politics of tribal Oman which resulted in the reassertion of control over the area by Sultan SA'ID BIN TAYMUR in 1955. Muhammad bin 'Abd Allah was succeeded as Imam by GHALIB BIN 'ALI al-HINA'I.

MUHAMMAD BIN 'ABD ALLAH al-SALIMI see 'ABD ALLAH BIN HUMAYD al-SALIMI

MUHAMMAD BIN 'ABD al-WAHHAB see MUWAHHIDUN

MUHAMMAD BIN HAMAD AL SHARQI (1908-1974). Paramount shaykh of the SHARQI tribe of al-FUJAYRAH for more than 40 years until his death, he was one of the leaders of the TRUCIAL STATES and the first Ruler of al-Fujayrah to be recognized as an independent (or Trucial) Ruler. He was also one of the founders of the UNITED ARAB EMIRATES (UAE) and served as an ex-officio member of the UAE Supreme Council of Rulers, the government's highest executive organ. At his death he was succeeded by his son, HAMAD BIN MUHAMMAD AL SHARQI, who at the time was serving as Minister of Agriculture and Fisheries in the UAE Cabinet.

al-MUHARRAQ. Second-largest island of the BAHRAYN archipelago and name of a town on the same island, the population of which was estimated at 40,000 to 50,000 in the mid-1970s. The intensively cultivated island is also the site of an international airport that was formerly a (British) Royal Air Force base. Since 1942, it has been connected to the capital, al-MANAMAH, on nearby al-Bahrayn Island, by a causeway.

MUHAWWALAH. Arabic term applied to those Arabs and/or Arab families who migrated to the Persian side of the Gulf at some point in the past and who subsequently returned to the Arab side. The appellation of muhawwalah frequently refers to persons of mixed Arab-Persian parentage, although the muhawwalah will often deny any Persian or SHI'I background.

MULLAH. A corruption of the Arabic word mawla, it is used to signify a religious leader, especially among the SHI'I sect.

MUSANDAM PENINSULA. The northernmost tip of land at the end of the RU'US al-JIBAL mountains that forms the southern edge of the Strait of HORMUZ. The Peninsula separates the Arabian (or, Persian) Gulf from what is known as the Gulf of OMAN. It is nearly severed from the mainland by KHAWR al-SHAMM (Elphinstone Inlet) and GHUBBAT al-GHAZIRAH (Malcolm's Inlet) and is connected only by the narrow Maqlab Isthmus. The name Musandam also applies to an island to the north of the Peninsula, approximately two miles in length, and culminating in the 100-foot cliff, Ra's Musandam, which marks the point where the two gulfs meet. All of Musandam is under the sovereignty of the Sultanate of OMAN and its inhabitants belong mainly to the SHIHUH tribe. The only town of any size is Kumzar. Frequently the word Musandam is applied to the entire Ru'us al-Jibal area as well.

MUSCAT (correctly: Masqat). Capital city of the Sultanate

of OMAN since 1784, with a population estimated at 10,000 in the mid-1970s. Located in a natural bowl formed by volcanic mountains, Muscat first gained prominence because of its well-protected harbor. The town was captured by the Portuguese in 1507 who held it until driven out by the IMAM of the YA'ARIBAH, Sultan bin Sayf, in 1650. Forts Jalali and Mirani, built by the Portuguese, still dominate the town and harbor. Tribesmen from the interior have repeatedly attacked the capital throughout its history, capturing it in 1868 and 1895 and threatening it in 1915. The accession of Sultan QABUS BIN SA'ID in 1970, followed by rapid expansion and sudden prosperity, signaled the eminent transformation of the medieval character of the old city with its picturesque walls and gates, mosques, old houses and suq.

The name also applies to the island which forms one side of the natural harbor and boasts a lighthouse as well as numerous names of ships that have called at Muscat whitewashed on its cliffs.

MUSCAT AND OMAN, SULTANATE OF see OMAN, SULTANATE OF

MUTAWWI' (plural: mutawi'ah). The religious leaders (equivalent of 'ULAMA' elsewhere in ISLAM) of the IBADI sect. During the 1868-1871 IMAMATE in MUSCAT, the mutawwi's were responsible for a fanatical application of Ibadi prohibitions and injunctions which included the harassment of the non-Ibadi population (including Indian merchants who were British subjects--a factor that contributed to Great Britain's hostility towards the short-lived Imamate). In the 1913-1920 revolt they forestalled the successful conclusion of negotiations between the Sultanate of OMAN and the tribal leaders of the interior until their major supporter, Imam SALIM BIN RASHID al-KHARUSI, was assassinated in 1920.

MUTLAQ al-MUTAYRI. SAUDI ARABIAN general in Eastern Arabia who led a joint Saudi-QASIMI expedition against the BATINAH Coast town of SHINAS (defended by the Sultanate of OMAN) in 1810, captured it, and continued to advance eastward along the coast to besiege the Omani capital at MUSCAT. Three years later, he plundered Muscat's neighboring city of MATRAH and waged a campaign into the eastern province of JA'LAN. He was killed in battle during an invasion of nearby al-SHARQIYYAH province in 1813.

MUWAHHIDUN (singular: muwahhid). An Arabic word meaning unitarians, referring to a fundamentalist variant of ISLAM often referred to in Western literature as Wahhabism, after its founder, Muhammad bin 'Abd al-Wahhab (1703-1792), a religious scholar of central Arabia who converted the leader of the Al Sa'ud dynasty of that area to his interpretation of the Hanbali school of Islamic jurisprudence. When the Saudi state was revived in the 20th century and eventually in an expanded version became the Kingdom of SAUDI ARABIA, special groups of Muwahhidun, called ikhwan (brotherhood), were established and officially encouraged to spread their beliefs throughout the Kingdom. As a result, many Western innovations have been slow to gain acceptance in Saudi Arabia, the role of women is still severely restricted, and many manifestations of the Islamic faith remain austere. Many members of the ruling families of 'AJMAN, QATAR, RA'S al-KHAYMAH, SHARJAH and UMM al-QAYWAYN, as well as several important tribes in the Sultanate of OMAN, have a traditional affinity with Eastern Arabian people who consider themselves muwahhidun.

- N -

NDFLOAG [National Democratic Front ...] see POPULAR FRONT FOR THE LIBERATION OF OMAN

NABAHINAH, AL (singular: Nabhani). A section of the Bani RIYAM tribe in the interior of OMAN formerly centered at the village of TANUF, now destroyed. The Al Nabahinah provided a medieval dynasty of IBADI Imams. In more recent times the tamimahs (paramount shaykhs) of the Bani Riyam came from the Al Nabahinah until 1959 when the incumbent, SULAYMAN BIN HIMYAR, fled the country after an unsuccessful revolt and the Sultan at that time, SA'ID BIN TAYMUR, prohibited the selection of a successor.

NABHAN, BANI see NABAHINAH, AL

al-NA'IM (singular: Na'imi, or Nu'aymi). A formerly powerful tribe in the Sultanate of OMAN, some sections of which are under the authority of the States of ABU DHABI, RA'S al-KHAYMAH, SHARJAH and 'AJMAN, as well. Other parts of the tribe have migrated to al-BAHRAYN, QATAR and the Eastern Province of SAUDI

ARABIA. The tribe is divided into three main sections: the Al Bu Khurayban (who are the principal inhabitants of the villages of al-Buraymi and Sa'arah in al-BURAYMI oasis, and who provide the tamimah or paramount shaykh for the tribe as well as the ruling family of 'Ajman); the Khawatir (who live in Hafit to the south and in Ra's al-Khaymah) and the Al Bu SHAMIS (who occupy al-Hamasah village in al-Buraymi). Both the Al Bu Khurayban and the Al Bu Shamis have badu (nomadic) sections which roam al-DHAHIRAH province, especially around DANK and al-QABIL. Over the years, the Al Bu Shamis have become increasingly estranged from the other two sections and are hence frequently classified as a separate tribe. The first two sections are at odds with the Al Bu FALAH, the Bani KA'B and the Bani QITAB. The Al Bu Shamis, correspondingly, have good relations with these tribes. The Na'im as a whole are SUNNI (and Hanbali in particular) and primarily GHAFIRI in politics. They became MUWAHHIDUN (Wahhabis) as a result of Saudi incursions in the area in the early 19th century and later were forcibly brought under the control of Shaykh ZAYID BIN KHALIFAH AL NUHAYYAN "The Great" of Abu Dhabi, until his death. Consequently, the Na'im proved to be among the strongest supporters and agents of the Saudis during the latter's occupation of al-Buraymi oasis (1952-1955).

NAJD (plural: nijad). Arabic term for highland or plateau. It is the name of the region of DHUFAR lying between the QARA Mountains and the RUB' al-KHALI desert and inhabited largely by the Bayt Kathir subdivision of the Al KATHIR tribe. The term also applies to an area of central Arabia which is the original home of the Al Sa'ud, the ruling family of SAUDI ARABIA.

NAKHL. An OMANI town of the Western HAJAR province about 20 miles south of BARKA (on the BATINAH Coast) at the base of the Jabal Nakhl, which separates Nakhl from the WADI SAMA'IL. It is inhabited by a number of minor tribes, the best known being the YA'ARIBAH which provided the dynasty of IBADI Imams from 1625 to 1737. Other tribes of the town include the Salimiyyin, Bani Harras and Kunud.

NAKHUDA. Persian word for captain. The term is used throughout the Gulf for the captain of a DHOW.

NATIONAL DEMOCRATIC FRONT FOR THE LIBERATION OF

THE OCCUPIED ARABIAN GULF see DHUFAR REBELLION; POPULAR FRONT FOR THE LIBERATION OF OMAN

NIZARI see 'ADNANI-YAMANI DIVISION

NIZWA. The largest town of interior OMAN, and its medieval capital, still regarded as the holy city of IBADISM. It became the capital of a revived Ibadi IMAMATE in 1913 until captured by the Sultanate of OMAN's military forces in 1955. Sultan SA'ID BIN TAYMUR entered NIZWA in December 1955, the first time in nearly a century that a Sultan had done so. The forces of the OMAN REVOLUTIONARY MOVEMENT (ORM) captured and held it briefly in 1957, but the town was soon placed permanently under the Sultan's wali (governor), who was also responsible for the nearby JABAL al-AKHDAR. Upper Nizwa (al-'ALAYAH) is GHAFIRI (mostly from the Bani RIYAM and Kunud tribes) and Lower Nizwa (al-SIFALAH) is HINAWI (mostly from the Al Bu SA'ID and Bani HINA tribes). The town is also noted for its huge Round Tower, a fort built by the YA'ARIBAH dynasty (17th and early 18th centuries) on solid rock, which rises high above the town and is nearly impregnable. A camp of the SULTAN's ARMED FORCES (SAF) is nearby.

NUHAYYAN, AL. The ruling family of the State of ABU DHABI. The Al Nuhayyan are from the Al Bu FALAH section of the Bani YAS tribe. All the rulers of Abu Dhabi since the shaykhdom was founded two centuries ago have been from this family. The most famous member was Shaykh ZAYID BIN KHALIFAH (r. 1855-1909) who was largely responsible for Abu Dhabi's becoming as powerful as its major rivals in the north, SHARJAH and RA'S al-KHAYMAH (dominated by QASIMI dynasties). With the formation of the UNITED ARAB EMIRATES (UAE), members of the Al Nuhayyan attained a number of important positions in the new state, including that of President (ZAYID BIN SULTAN, the Ruler of Abu Dhabi), and the heads of several ministries.

- O -

OAPEC see ORGANIZATION OF ARAB PETROLEUM EXPORTING COUNTRIES

OPEC see ORGANIZATION OF PETROLEUM EXPORTING COUNTRIES

ORM see OMAN REVOLUTIONARY MOVEMENT

OASIS. Practically any place in a desert area where there is sufficient water for agricultural production is an oasis. In Eastern Arabia, this production is generally confined to date palms, lucerne, wheat, mangoes, bananas, oranges and limes. Larger oases are often composed of a number of different settlements separated by desert, such as al-BURAYMI or al-LIWA. The inhabitants are usually drawn from sections of badu (nomad) tribes that have settled. Nomadic sections of these tribes often own date gardens in the oasis and periodically camp there to harvest them. The oases can be important politically as reference points on an otherwise featureless landscape (in the manner that al-Buraymi served as the focal point of SAUDI claims in Eastern Arabia). They may also perform the role of social indicators of heritage (in the manner that ruling families of the Gulf frequently trace their descendants back to certain oases). Many of the townspeople along the Gulf coast frequent the inland oases which serve as weekend and summer retreats. The oasis also serves as the link between the HADR or settled areas of the coast and the badu or nomadic tribes of the desert interior. The Arabic word for oasis is "wahah" (plural: wahat).

OIL EXPLORATION. The earliest oil related activities in eastern Arabia included an exploration party by D'Arcy Exploration Co. (a wholly-owned subsidiary of Anglo-Persian Oil Co., later renamed British Petroleum or BP) in the interior of OMAN and the activities of Frank Holmes in al-BAHRAYN on behalf of Eastern and General Syndicate. The Oman expedition was unsuccessful and in 1927 the Bahrayn concession was relinquished to Gulf Oil, which in turn gave it to Standard Oil of California. Due to an agreement between the Ruler of al-Bahrayn and the British, which required that the concessionaires be British, Standard founded BAHRAIN PETROLEUM CO. (BAPCO) in Canada in 1930 and then brought in the Texas Co. (Texaco) as an equal partner. Oil was discovered in 1932 and a refinery built in 1937.

Elsewhere in the area, successful exploration proceeded more slowly. QATAR first granted a concession to QATAR PETROLEUM CO. (QPC; a subsidiary of Iraq Petroleum Co.) in 1935; oil was discovered three years later but World War II prevented production until 1949. To the south, Iraq Petroleum Co. (IPC) had formed Petroleum Concessions Ltd. to acquire exploration rights (beginning in 1937) with the Sultanate of OMAN, DUBAY, SHARJAH, DHUFAR (part of Oman) and later RA'S al-KHAYMAH, ABU DHABI, KALBAH, and 'AJMAN. But problems in security and the Second World War prevented significant activity. Abu Dhabi led what became a 1960s boom with exports beginning in 1962. Oil was discovered in Oman by PETROLEUM DEVELOPMENT (OMAN) LTD. (PDO) in 1964, in Dubay by DUBAI PETROLEUM CO. in 1966 and in SHARJAH by Buttes Oil and Gas in 1969.

The original pattern of British and American concessions covering entire states was first altered in the 1950s with the development of off-shore concessions, which have since proved particularly successful in Abu Dhabi, Dubay, Sharjah, and Qatar. By the 1960s, arrangements between the concessionaires and the concession-granting states had been modified, with increased payments going to the governments of the producing states; eventually, partnership arrangements were made between the companies and these states. When the original concession-holders relinquished unproductive territory (according to the terms of the old concessions), a pattern emerged whereby independent companies took over exploration and operated strictly for the states concerned. American, French, Italian, German and particularly Japanese companies were active in this regard. Another development was increasing host-state ownership of original operators (such as BAPCO, QPC and PDO) themselves.

OMAN [see also following entries]. The extreme eastern part of the Arabian Peninsula. Today the term "Oman" (the correct transliteration from the Arabic is 'Uman) is generally restricted to the territory of the Sultanate of OMAN, although in geographical terms, it includes the territory of the UNITED ARAB EMIRATES (UAE; also called Peninsular Oman and formerly known as the TRUCIAL COAST or Trucial Oman) and excludes DHUFAR, the southern province of the Sultanate. Geographical Oman is surrounded on three sides by water (the Arabian Gulf in the north, the Gulf of OMAN in the east and the Arabian Sea in the south) and on the western side by the vast sandy expanse of the RUB' al-KHALI (Empty Quarter).

A major feature of the area is the long, unbroken beaches along the Gulf (i. e., the former Trucial Coast) and along the Gulf of Oman (known as the BATINAH Coast). From near the eastern point of land (RA'S al-HADD), the HAJAR mountain range extends westward and parallel to the shoreline, until it turns due north and becomes the RU'US al-JIBAL, and culminating in Ra's MUSANDAM. It separates the former Trucial Coast (now the western coast of the UAE) from the Batinah Coast as well as the Arabian Gulf from the Gulf of Oman. The Hajar's highest massif is the JABAL al-AKHDAR in the center of the range, reaching a height of 10,000 feet. Behind the Hajar, a central inhabited plateau gently slopes down to the Rub' al-Khali desert. The largest settlements of the coast include ABU DHABI, DUBAY, SHARJAH, RA'S al-KHAYMAH, SUHAR, MATRAH, MUSCAT and SUR. Inland, the more important settlements include al-BURAYMI, 'IBRI, NIZWA, BAHLA, SAMA'IL and al-RUSTAQ.

At frequent intervals, Oman has been closely linked with nearby Persia (Iran). When its first Arab inhabitants arrived from Yemen in the second century B.C., they had to win their settlements by defeating the Persian army along the coast. These Arabs settled principally in the interior so that when the first Europeans (the Portuguese) arrived in the 16th century, the coast was still subject to the Persian King of HORMUZ. The Portuguese proceeded to dominate the coast until driven out in the mid-17th century, and except for a brief period in the mid-18th century when the area was subject once again to a Persian invasion, most of Oman has remained an independent country.

There has been a wide gap between the isolated region of the interior--Arab, Islamic and split between SUNNISM and IBADISM--and the more accessible and outward-looking coastal areas--inhabited by large numbers of non-Arab immigrants from Iran, Pakistan, India and Africa, as well as indigenous Arabs. Although the coastline was well known for centuries (a British Residency was established in Muscat in 1800), the interior was late in being explored. The first such explorers were two lieutenants of the Royal Navy, J. R. WELLSTED and F. Whitelock, in 1835-1836 (they were also the first Europeans to set foot on the Jabal al-Akhdar). The next to journey inland was the French botanist Pierre Martin Aucher-Eloy, two years later. The first excursion into Peninsular Oman was made by Captain Atkins HAMERTON of the Bombay Army, who traveled from Sharjah to al-Buraymi and then through the WADI al-JIZZI to Suhar in 1840. In 1845, Lt. C. S. D. Cole of the Indian Navy landed on the coast near JA'LAN in the south and made his way overland to Nizwa and the Jabal al-Akhdar and on to Muscat. Subsequently, travel into the interior became much more difficult because of political anarchy in the area and the only European to do much exploring during the remainder of the 19th century was the Political Agent at Muscat, Samuel B. MILES.

OMAN, GULF OF. The extension of the Indian Ocean that separates the Arabian Gulf from the Arabian Sea. The Gulf of Oman is roughly triangular-shaped with the Arabian Sea to the east, the Iranian and Pakistani coast to the north, and the OMAN coast of the Arabian Peninsula to the south. Its western edge is the Strait of HORMUZ, which links the two Gulfs.

OMAN, SULTANATE OF. The political territory ruled by the Al Bu SA'ID dynasty since 1744. At various times, this has included all of geographical OMAN except for Peninsular Oman or the TRUCIAL COAST, as well as al-BAHRAYN, HORMUZ and Bandar 'Abbas on the Persian coast, GWADAR on the Pakistan Coast, ZANZIBAR and portions of the East African littoral. The greatest period of Sultanate expansion was under Sultan SA'ID BIN SULTAN THE GREAT (r. 1807-1856). At other times, the territory consisted of little more than the MUSCAT/MATRAH area and a few towns along the BATINAH coast. In the mid-20th century, the territory of the Sultanate included the geographical provinces of al-Batinah, al-DHAHIRAH (al-Zahirah), al-HAJAR (Eastern and Western), JA'LAN, MUSANDAM, al-SHARQIYYAH, and DHUFAR.

The Sultanate has often been contrasted with the IMAMATE of Oman, an institution out of which the Sultanate grew and which has existed parallel with the Sultanate at various periods during the last two centuries. As a result of his success in driving the Persian invaders out of Oman in 1744, AHMAD BIN SA'ID AL BU SA'ID was elected IBADI Imam. Ahmad began a long line of familial succession, which over time dropped the title of Imam and became known first as "Sayyids" and then as Sultans. With the death of Sultan SA'ID BIN SULTAN in 1856 and the diminishing fortunes of the Sultanate thereafter, the British (through the Government of India) felt compelled to take a more active role in Sultanate affairs. By the early 20th century, they had assumed a predominant role in the foreign affairs and internal administration of the nominally independent country.

The state was rent by rebellion during the Imamate of 'AZZAN BIN QAYS (who ruled Muscat as Imam and not Sultan from 1868 to 1871) and during the Sultanate of FAYSAL BIN TURKI (r. 1888-1913). The adoption of a modus vivendi and autonomy for the interior was gained during the reign of TAYMUR BIN FAYSAL (r. 1913-1931) when the Agreement of al-SIB was signed in 1920. Taymur was succeeded in 1932 by his son, SA'ID BIN TAYMUR, who reunited the coast and interior in 1955, suppressed another rebellion in the late 1950s and was eventually (in 1970) deposed by his son, QABUS BIN SA'ID, because of his inability to cope effectively with the DHUFAR REBELLION and the myriad problems of social and economic growth made possible by the oil revenues which began to accrue after 1967. After 1970, the Sultanate underwent drastic transformation, bursting out of its isolation with an ambitious development program financed by increasing oil revenues, which in the mid-1970s approximated $1 billion annually.

OMAN PROVINCE. The region of geographical Oman (also called Oman Proper) lying to the interior of the HAJAR Mountain Range, and which is politically part of the Sultanate of OMAN. Its boundaries are formed by the JABAL al-AKHDAR massif of the HAJAR Range in the east and the RUB' al-KHALI desert in the west. To the north, Oman Proper gives way to al-DHAHIRAH province somewhat south of 'IBRI; to the south, Oman Proper extends to al-SHARQIYYAH province and the WAHIBAH SANDS.

This was the first area occupied by the Arab migrations from the YEMEN in the A. D. 100's and has always been the focal point of Omani culture and history. Its towns of NIZWA, BAHLA and Jabrin have all at one time or another served as the capital of the IBADI IMAMATE. Major tribes of the area include the Bani HINA, the Bani RIYAM, the Bani RUWAHAH, the Al Bu SA'ID and the 'IBRIYYIN. In the 20th century, Oman Proper has at times been semi-independent of the Sultanate; from 1913 to 1955 it was the capital of an Imamate.

OMAN REVOLUTIONARY MOVEMENT (ORM). Developed in

the mid-1950s by a secularization of the traditional IBADI IMAMATE of interior OMAN. Since 1913, part of Oman had been semi-independent of the Sultanate of OMAN, a state of affairs acknowledged in the Agreement of al-SIB (1920), which recognized the domination of the interior by a kind of tribal anarchy (albeit loosely controlled by an Imam). In 1954, GHALIB BIN 'ALI al-HINA'I succeeded MUHAMMAD BIN 'ABD ALLAH al-KHALILI as Imam. A year later, a Saudi police detachment which had been in al-BURAYMI since 1952 and had been providing arms and cash to the new Imam and his principal supporters, was driven out of the oasis and an armed force of the Sultanate occupied the Imamate capital at NIZWA. Ghalib bin 'Ali abdicated and his brother, TALIB BIN 'ALI, fled to al-DAMMAM in SAUDI ARABIA, where he proceeded to train an army. Of the two major tribal supporters of the movement, SULAYMAN BIN HIMYAR of the Bani RIYAM chose to make his peace with the Sultan while SALIH BIN 'ISA of the HIRTH fled to ZANZIBAR and then to Egypt. By 1957 Talib's army was prepared; he entered Oman secretly and engaged the Sultanate's military forces at Bilad Sayt (near BAHLA). When Sulayman bin Himyar joined Talib and Ghalib, the rebels were able to capture and briefly hold Nizwa before a combined Sultanate-British operation drove them up on the JABAL al-AKHDAR mountain massif. There they remained until forced to flee when the mountain was captured by government forces in early 1959. The rebel triumvirate then made their headquarters in Egypt, and with the help of the Egyptians, the Saudis and later the Iraqis, made the "question of Oman" the basis for an attack on British "colonialism" within the forums of the Arab League and the United Nations.

ORGANIZATION OF ARAB PETROLEUM EXPORTING COUNTRIES (OAPEC). Founded in 1968 to promote the interests of the Arab members of the more inclusive Organization of Petroleum Exporting Countries (OPEC). It was originally composed of the more traditional Arab producers (al-KUWAYT, SAUDI ARABIA and Libya) but following the 1969 revolution in Libya, expanded to include Algeria, al-BAHRAYN, Egypt, Iraq, QATAR, Syria, ABU DHABI and DUBAY. The last-named state withdrew from OAPEC in the early 1970s when the organization chose to finance a multi-million drydock scheme in al-Bahrayn instead of Dubay. The Sultanate of OMAN is not a member of either OAPEC or OPEC.

It should be noted that contrary to popular myth, the "Arab oil boycott" of the United States, Holland and Portugal and the more generalized productional cutbacks applied during the October War of 1973 and for a period afterwards (the boycott came to an end on March 18, 1974) were not OAPEC operations. The decisions to implement these and related policies were made independently and in some instances quite differently by individual Arab ministers of petroleum. Some OAPEC members, most notably Iraq, refused to reduce production.

ORGANIZATION OF PETROLEUM EXPORTING COUNTRIES (OPEC). An international organization composed of 13 oil-exporting, Third World countries, including QATAR and the UNITED ARAB EMIRATES. OPEC was founded in 1960 to assure its members a stable price for their petroleum; headquarters were subsequently established in Vienna. Pricing decisions taken by OPEC affect other oil-producing states in Eastern Arabia through most-favored-nation concession clauses that guarantee the host governments the same price for their oil as the OPEC members receive. See also preceding entry.

ORMUZ see HORMUZ

OTTAVI, PAUL. French Consul at MUSCAT from 1894 to 1901. Ottavi opened his government's consulate, which functioned only until 1905. He was the principal agent of the French challenge to British supremacy in the Sultanate of OMAN. His efforts in that direction included an attempt to acquire French rights to a coaling station near Muscat at BANDAR Jissah, the permission he extended to DHOWS engaged in the slave trade to hoist the French flag, and his encouragement of French arms merchants in the sale of their wares in Muscat. A strong British admonition to Sultan FAYSAL BIN TURKI (r. 1888-1913) blocked the coaling station deal, and multilateral international action resolved the other two issues. The house that Ottavi occupied in Muscat is still known as Bayt Faransi (French House) although no Frenchman has occupied it since 1905.

- P -

PDO see PETROLEUM DEVELOPMENT (OMAN) LTD.

PFLO see POPULAR FRONT FOR THE LIBERATION OF OMAN

PFLOAG see POPULAR FRONT FOR THE LIBERATION OF OMAN

PRPG see POLITICAL RESIDENT IN THE PERSIAN GULF

PALGRAVE, WILLIAM. A 19th-century British explorer of Arabia. Palgrave had once been in the Bombay Army but later became a member of the Society of Jesus. Although the reasons for his travels through Arabia are somewhat obscure, he apparently undertook them for the French government. He left Gaza in May 1862 and traveled through Jabal Shammar, Riyadh, Qatif, al-DAWHAH, SHARJAH, SUHAR and MUSCAT. In the spring of 1863 he left Arabia and returned to Syria by way of BUSHIRE. His account of these travels was published as Narrative of a Year's Journey through Central and Eastern Arabia (London, 1865). Because of inaccuracies and mistakes in his notes of the journey, many scholars have doubted their authenticity.

PATHANS. A people of Afghanistan and northern Pakistan. Large numbers of Pathans have immigrated to the oil-producing states of Eastern Arabia in search of jobs. Typically, a Pathan is engaged in occupations requiring long and hard labor such as construction. On the other hand, many of them disdain port work (such as that of longshoremen) as beneath their dignity. Like most other immigrant groups, their main purpose for being in the area is generally to save a maximum amount of money in as short a span of time as possible--two years is the average stay of most of the unskilled Pathans, who comprise the majority of the total--after which they tend to return to their original homes.

PEARLING. Eastern Arabia has been noted for its pearls since recorded history and pearling was for centuries the major occupation in the area. The major pearling banks are located in the area between the QATAR Peninsula and the western coast of the UNITED ARAB EMIRATES (UAE). In the early 20th century, when pearling was at its zenith, thousands of divers worked the banks during the season from early June to late September. However, the double impact of the introduction of Japanese cultured pearls to the world market and the global recession of the 1930s dealt the industry a blow from which it has never recovered. Pearling was especially important for the island State of al-BAHRAYN, where upwards of 20,000 men were dependent on the annual harvest. The longtime British Adviser to al-Bahrayn, Sir Charles BELGRAVE, once suggested that al-Bahrayn advertise its close relationship with the pearl by stamping outgoing letters with the phrase, "Drape your girls in Bahrain pearls."

PELLY, LEWIS. Political officer of the Government of India in the latter half of the 19th century. Pelly was Political Agent in ZANZIBAR in 1860, then became officiating POLITICAL RESIDENT IN THE PERSIAN GULF in 1861. His position was made permanent in 1862 and he held it until 1872. Pelly understood his role in the Gulf as that of an agent of Western civilization, and he consequently urged the expansion and assimilation of European ideas and practices throughout the region. Although narrow-minded in his administration of the Gulf, his practices and philosophy were supported by his superior, Sir Bartle Frere, the Governor of Bombay. His attitude was manifest in his strong-armed action against MUWAHHIDUN (Wahhabi) incursions into al-DAMMAM and OMAN. His mistaken belief that the reign of 'AZZAN BIN QAYS (r. 1868-1871) in MUSCAT was no more than a Muwahhidun régime made for the withholding of British recognition and the ZANZIBAR SUBSIDY, which resulted in the régime's collapse. Another consequence of Pelly's service in the Gulf was the official subordination of the Political Agent at Muscat to the Resident in the Gulf, a necessity brought about by Pelly's feuding with various Muscat agents over what he considered to be proper policy.

PERSIAN GULF see ARABIAN GULF

PETROLEUM DEVELOPMENT (OMAN) LTD. (PDO). The major oil concession operator in the Sultanate of OMAN, and as of 1975 the only oil producer in that country. Originally a subsidiary of the Iraq Petroleum Co. (IPC), the concession in OMAN dates back to 1937 and exploration began in earnest in 1954. Most of the IPC partners withdrew in 1960 following the lack of drilling success, leaving only Royal Dutch-Shell and Participation and Explorations Corp. (Partex; the Gulbenkian interest). Oil was finally discovered at FAHUD in 1964 and oil exports began in 1967. Petroleum was also discovered at Yibal and Natih, all three locations being on the edge of the RUB' al-KHALI desert. A pipeline was built from Fahud through the WADI SAMA'IL to the company's headquarters and oil terminal at Mina' al-Fahal (formerly known as Sayh al-Malih and located just west of MATRAH). In 1975, ownership of PDO was divided among the Sultanate of Oman (60%), Royal Dutch-Shell (34%), Compagnie Française des Pétroles (4%) and Partex (2%). PDO also reacquired the concession for DHUFAR province in 1969 where it has continued exploration. The company's incursion into the interior of Oman in 1954 was an important factor in the subsequent rebellion by the OMAN REVOLUTIONARY MOVEMENT (ORM). All oil produced up to 1975 was in the territory of the DURU' tribe. Other concessions have been granted to Wintershall A. G. (off the BATINAH Coast), Oman Sun Oil (an American-Canadian-German consortium, in the Gulf of MASIRAH), and Elf-ERAP (off the MUSANDAM Peninsula).

PHILBY, H. ST. JOHN B. (1885-1960). A 20th-century British diplomat turned traveler and writer. He joined the Indian Political Service in 1907 and served in Iraq from 1915 to 1917. In 1917, he was sent to secure the neutrality of a rising shaykh of central Arabia, 'Abd al-'Aziz bin 'Abd al-Rahman Al Sa'ud, commonly known as Ibn Sa'ud. In the process he crossed the Arabian Peninsula from al-KUWAYT to Jiddah, a journey that marked the beginning of a long and intimate relationship with Arabia. After subsequently serving in Iraq and Transjordan, he resigned from British officialdom in protest over his government's policy in the area and settled in Jiddah. He became a close adviser to King 'Abd al-'Aziz. Moreover, he converted to Islam and took a Muslim wife (in addition to his English spouse). Philby became a renowned explorer of Arabia, particularly with his 1932 crossing of the RUB' al-KHALI desert (the second European to accomplish this feat), and the author of numerous books on Arabia. After the death of King 'Abd al-'Aziz in 1953, he was temporarily banished from SAUDI ARABIA and died in Beirut in 1960. His son Kim, a member of the British intelligence establishment, defected to the Soviet Union in 1963.

PHILLIPS, WENDELL (1921-1975). American maverick oilman and amateur archeologist. He first entered OMAN in the late 1950s after his archeological expedition to the YEMEN was driven out of the country by soldiers of the IMAM. In Oman, he became a confidant of Sultan SA'ID BIN TAYMUR AL BU SA'ID, with whom he spent considerable time in SALALAH. The Sultan eventually granted him an oil concession for the province of DHUFAR. Although it proved to be commercially unproductive, Phillips went on to acquire other, more lucrative, concessions elsewhere. An attempt to receive another concession from Sultan QABUS BIN SA'ID in 1971 ended in failure when Phillips was refused entry to the Sultanate. He has authored two books on the country (Oman: A History and Unknown Oman), both of which received considerable criticism from people familiar with the Sultanate.

PIRACY. Attacks by ships of one tribe against those of another was a traditional feature of maritime activity in Eastern Arabia prior to the ongoing contact of these states with various European countries. The epithet "piracy," however, originated with Western--primarily Portuguese, Dutch, French and English--trading concerns in the area who interpreted the maritime warfare of the area as acts of piracy aimed at plundering European commercial vessels. Consequently, the name "Pirate Coast" was applied to the southern coast of the Gulf (whose tribes were extensively engaged in the activity) and the British began to exert naval force to protect their shipping. The ports of KHAWR FAKKAN and RA'S al-KHAYMAH (then known as JULFAR), the principal headquarters of the QASIMI tribe, were captured and destroyed in 1819. British pressure induced the ruling shaykhs of the "Pirate Coast" to sign a GENERAL TREATY OF PEACE in 1820, restricting the use of force offshore, and eventually the Treaty of Perpetual MARITIME PEACE was promulgated in 1853 whereby the states of the area renounced the use of maritime force altogether and acknowledged British responsibility for keeping the peace at sea. The "Pirate" Coast thereafter became known as the "TRUCIAL" COAST.

POLITICAL RESIDENT IN THE PERSIAN GULF (PRPG). The British official of the Government of India who was responsible for the implementation of policy in the GULF and Eastern Arabia. Under the PRPG was a network of Political Agents and Officers located at one time or another in MUSCAT, Bandar 'Abbas, SHARJAH, DUBAY, ABU DHABI, al-DAWHAH (QATAR), al-MANAMAH (al-BAHRAYN), al-KUWAYT and al-Basrah (Iraq). The residency itself was located in BUSHIRE on the

Iranian coast until the late 1940s, when it was transferred to al-Manamah. With the official British withdrawal in 1971 and the evolution of the smaller states of the area from British-protected status to fully independent states, the post of PRPG was abolished. Some of the more notable Residents included Lewis PELLY, Sir Percy COX and Sir Arnold Wilson; the last Resident was Sir Geoffrey Arthur. The Resident from 1961 to 1965, Sir William LUCE, returned as Representative in the Gulf in 1970. In that capacity he was the principal British official responsible for negotiating an end to the special British treaty relationship with the nine emirates of Eastern Arabia.

POPULAR FRONT FOR THE LIBERATION OF OMAN (PFLO). The rebel organization that operated in DHUFAR province of the Sultanate of OMAN during the latter stages of the DHUFAR REBELLION. It grew out of the nationalist Dhufar Liberation Front (DLF) which had launched the rebellion in the early 1960s. At the DLF's conference at Hamrin (a village in western Dhufar) in 1968, the radical wing of rebels managed to gain control of the movement and rename it the Popular Front for the Liberation of the Occupied Arabian Gulf (PFLOAG). When this organization absorbed the National Democratic Front for the Liberation of Oman and the Arabian Gulf (NDFLOAG) in late 1970, it assumed a second new name: Popular Front for the Liberation of Oman and the Arabian Gulf, referred to by the same acronym PFLOAG. After the accession of Sultan QABUS BIN SA'ID in July 1970, the early successes of the rebellion began to wane. By the summer of 1974, a series of rebel setbacks led to a schism within PFLOAG, with members from the GULF emirates expressing a desire to transform the organization into a legitimate political party that would work within the system, while the Dhufari members argued in favor of continuing the rebellion. As a result of this cleavage, the latter faction reorganized under the PFLO banner. One reason for the PFLO's lack of success during its first year was its inability to attract sufficient support from such states as the Soviet Union, the People's Republic of China and the People's Democratic Republic of Yemen, which PFLOAG had enjoyed.

POPULAR FRONT FOR THE LIBERATION OF OMAN AND THE ARABIAN GULF see DHUFAR REBELLION; POPULAR FRONT FOR THE LIBERATION OF OMAN

POPULAR FRONT FOR THE LIBERATION OF THE OCCUPIED ARABIAN GULF see POPULAR FRONT FOR THE LIBERATION OF OMAN

PORTUGUESE IN EASTERN ARABIA. A Portuguese fleet under the leadership of Affonso d'Albuquerque appeared off OMAN in 1507 and moved up the coast, sacking the towns of QALHAT, QURIYAT, MUSCAT, SUHAR and KHAWR FAKKAN. Although these early Europeans were unable to conquer HORMUZ, the Kingdom of which ruled the Omani seaports at that time, another fleet returned in 1515, conquered Hormuz and established permanent garrisons in the aforementioned towns. The Portuguese maintained a weak control over this area for the next century and a half despite incursions by the Ottoman navy and the IMAMATE of the interior. The Portuguese advance into the GULF was buttressed by the construction of forts at al-BAHRAYN, JULFAR (present-day RA'S al-KHAYMAH), and KHASAB. However, growing competition from England and Holland, coupled with the increasing power of Persia, entailed a decline in Portuguese fortunes in the area, and by 1650 the YA'ARIBAH dynasty of Imams in Oman had recaptured Muscat, the last Portuguese stronghold in Arabia. Remnants of the lengthy Portuguese presence in the area can be seen in al-Bahrayn and MATRAH (where Portuguese forts still stand) and especially in Muscat, where the twin forts of Jalali and Mirani (completed in 1587 and 1588) overlook the harbor; where Burj Kabrita (Cabretta), a tower on the town walls, commemorates its Portuguese defender in the siege of 1650; and where one of the town's old houses, Bayt Gharayza (Greiza) derives its name from the old Portuguese cathedral that once stood on the same spot (gharayza being the Arabic equivalent of the Portuguese word for church).

- Q -

QPC see QATAR PETROLEUM CO.

al-QABIL. The name of two OMANI settlements. The larger is located in al-SHARQIYYAH province and is the headquarters of the HIRTH tribe, the most important tribe of that area. However, because of a lack of adequate rainfall since the 1940s, cultivation in the area has been severely hampered and many of its people have left.

The other Qabil is located some distance away at the southern tip of the Jabal Hafit mountain in al-DHAHIRAH province a few miles south of al-BURAYMI. Most of its inhabitants are from the NA'IM tribe.

QABUS BIN SA'ID AL BU SA'ID. The 14th Ruler of the Al Bu Sa'id dynasty of OMAN. Sultan Qabus was born in SALALAH, DHUFAR, in 1940 to a QARA mother. His father, Sultan SA'ID BIN TAYMUR, arranged for Qabus' education at Sandhurst Military Academy in England. Following graduation and a brief period of service as an officer with the British Army of the Rhine in West Germany, Qabus returned to Salalah where he was kept under virtual house arrest by his father until 1970, when Sa'id was deposed in a coup d'état on July 23rd and Qabus replaced him as Sultan. A week later, Qabus visited MUSCAT for the first time and promised a complete change from the isolationist, restrictive policies of his father. Subsequently, the Sultanate embarked on an ambitious program of socio-economic development.

QADI (plural: qudah). A judge or magistrate in Islamic jurisprudence. Generally the responsibility of a qadi is limited to the SHARI'AH (Islamic law), including issues of personal status such as marriage, divorce, inheritance and child care. In addition, a qadi usually handles only cases involving members of the same school of Islamic jurisprudence (i. e., either Hanafi, Hanbali, Maliki, or Shafi'i). In the Sultanate of OMAN, where there are probably more qadis than in all the Eastern Arabian emirates combined, a qadi is generally assigned to each wali (governor) and a court of appeals from qadis' decisions exists in MUSCAT.

QAHTANI see 'ADNANI-YAMANI DIVISION

QALHAT. A small fishing village on the Gulf of OMAN approximately 15 miles to the northwest of SUR. Qalhat is one of the oldest villages in OMAN and contains some of the most ancient ruins in Eastern Arabia. Part of the first Arab migration to Oman came to Qalhat by sea in the second century B. C. The settlement became a port of the Kings of HORMUZ ca. A. D. 1270, and soon after was visited by both Marco Polo and Ibn Battutah. It was the first Omani port visited by the PORTUGUESE under Affonso d'Albuquerque in 1507 (thus becoming the first part of Eastern Arabia visited by Europeans since the time of Alexander the Great). Qalhat's harbor silted up several centuries ago and as a result, the village has greatly diminished in size and importance.

QAMAR see JABAL QAMAR

QARA (singular: Qarawi). One of the several peoples who speak a non-Arabic language as their primary tongue and inhabit DHUFAR (the others being the MAHRA, the Shera, the Batahirah and, by some accounts, the original Harasis). They are generally thought to be descended from the original South Arabian nations and to have migrated to Dhufar about a thousand years ago, moving into the Qara and Qamar Mountains and dispossessing the original inhabitants, the Shera. Often called jibalis (Arabic for mountain dwellers), the Qara are mostly sedentary herdsmen of goats and a small local cattle; some are cave-dwellers. They are divided into a number of sections, called bayts. Disaffected by the paternalistic policies of the Sultan of Oman, SA'ID BIN TAYMUR, they provided the backbone of the DHUFAR REBELLION. The mother of Sultan QABUS BIN SA'ID is a Qara from the Bayt Ma'ashani section of Taqah (a small town along the coast to the east of SALALAH).

QARAMITAH (singular: Qarmati). A fundamentalist Islamic sect which arose in Iraq in the late A. D. 800's. The Qaramitah (also known as Qarmatians or Carmathians) preached a return to the "pure" form of Islam and backed their beliefs with the sword, ravaging Iraq and Syria before being driven into central Arabia and al-BAHRAYN. There they were accepted by the badu (nomadic) tribes and even captured the sacred Black Stone of Islam during a raid on the Holy City of Mecca in 930. The rise of the MUWAHHIDUN (Unitarians; "Wahhabis") under Saudi patronage encouraged many European observers to note that the movement was similar to the Qaramitah.

QASIMI see QAWASIM

QATAR. An independent state and peninsula of the same name on the Arab side of the GULF. The peninsula is approximately 100 miles long and encompasses 4000 square miles. In the mid-1970s the state had an estimated population of 170, 000, which included indigenous

Arabs as well as Iranian, Indian, Pakistani and Western immigrants. The State of Qatar has been fully independent since 1971, prior to which it was a British protected-state. Its Ruler is a shaykh of the Al THANI family and the capital is al-DAWHAH (also, Doha) on the eastern side of the peninsula. One of the largest cities in Eastern Arabia, al-Dawhah was the site of an Ottoman garrison functioning in the late 19th century. Other major towns include the port settlement of Khawr to the north of al-Dawhah, the center of petroleum production at DUKHAN (on the western side of the peninsula), and the oil terminal and industrial site of UMM SA'ID (to the south of al-Dawhah).

A flourishing pre-historic culture is indicated by the prevalence of ancient burial mounds in the western part of the state. The peninsula was relatively unknown to the West until the 20th century: the first European to explore its interior was Hermann Burchardt in 1904. Before the discovery of oil in 1949, Qatar's main income came from the nearby pearl banks as well as badu (nomadic) pursuits. The major oil operations are QATAR PETROLEUM CO. (QPC) and Shell Co. of Qatar.

Because the ruling family and most of the local population of Qatar share the same MUWAHHIDUN creed of SUNNI Islam with neighboring SAUDI ARABIA, relations between the two countries have always been close (even though troubled at times in the past as a result of boundary disputes in the KHAWR al-'UDAYD area). Relations with nearby al-BAHRAYN, the ruling family of which once controlled large areas of Qatar, have traditionally been less cordial. In the 20th century many of the tensions between the two states have remained volatile; this is due to acute differences as to which state is sovereign over al-ZUBARAH, a village settlement on the northwest edge of the peninsula, and the HAWAR Islands, which lie between the two states.

QATAR PETROLEUM CO. (QPC). The onshore oil producer in the State of QATAR. Originally founded under the name of Petroleum Development (Qatar) Ltd. as a subsidiary of Iraq Petroleum Co. (IPC), the company obtained a concession in 1935 and discovered oil three years later. Interrupted by World War II, production did not commence until 1949. The name of the company was changed to its present form in 1953. Despite much effort, the only field discovered remains one at DUKHAN (on the western coast) from which the oil is pumped via a 50-mile pipeline to a terminal at UMM SA'ID (on the eastern coast). Territory relinquished by QPC was eventually granted in a concession to Continental Oil of Qatar.

Offshore operations had been conducted under a concession granted to the Shell Co. of Qatar in 1952. Oil was finally discovered after ten years of effort and the expenditure of £16 million sterling by the company. Production commenced in 1965. Continental Oil of Qatar also received an offshore concession for territories relinquished by Shell in 1963. In 1974, the government acquired a 60 per cent ownership in both QPC and Shell. See also OIL EXPLORATION.

QAWASIM [Jawasim] (singular: Qasimi, often pronounced "Jasimi"). An important tribe that provides the ruling families of the states of SHARJAH and RA'S al-KHAYMAH. The first Western contact with the Qawasim came through their reputation as pirates in the area. To deal with this problem, Great Britain was compelled to become more and more involved with the region and in 1819 a British force conquered the Qasimi capital of Ra's al-Khaymah (then known as JULFAR). The other Qasimi center at Sharjah was later to become headquarters for the British presence on the TRUCIAL COAST. The former predominant status of the Qawasim has not been forgotten by members of the tribe and members of the ruling households of Sharjah and Ra's al-Khaymah have been resentful of the stronger role that the heads of the Bani YAS tribe of ABU DHABI and DUBAY have been given in the UNITED ARAB EMIRATES (UAE). An important Ruler of Sharjah and member of the family in the early 19th century was SULTAN BIN SAQR. More recent Rulers have been SAQR BIN SULTAN (r. 1951-1965), KHALID BIN MUHAMMAD (r. 1965-1972) and SULTAN BIN MUHAMMAD (r. 1972-).

QITAB, BANI (singular: Qitbi). A tribe of northern OMAN divided into two major sections. One is centered around al-DHAYD in the State of SHARJAH; the other is located at Aflaj Bani Qitab (south of DANK) in al-DHAHIRAH province in the Sultanate of OMAN. There is also a badu (nomadic) section around al-BURAYMI whom SAUDI ARABIA claimed as its subjects in the 1950s. The tribe is SUNNI (and Hanbali in matters of Islamic law) and GHAFIRI in politics. The tribe has long been allied to the Bani KA'B.

THE QUOINS see SALAMAH WA-BINATUHA

QURIYAT. A port and fishing village situated on the Gulf of OMAN approximately 30 miles southeast of MUSCAT. As the coast is sheer on both sides of Quriyat, the village can be reached only by land via a narrow, twisting wadi. Quriyat was the first Omani city to resist the occupation of the PORTUGUESE in 1507 and consequently was ordered destroyed by the leader of the Portuguese fleet, Affonso d'Albuquerque.

- R -

RAFIQ (plural: rufaqa'). Arabic word for companion or escort. Used in tribal areas to denote the member of a tribe who accompanies outsiders across tribal territory and who thereby insures the outsider's safety against harm to himself or his property. Occasionally the words rabi' or khatir are used as a substitute for rafiq.

RAMLAH (plural: rimal). Arabic term for sand or a sandy region. In Eastern Arabia, the word is frequently used as a place name, as in the Ramlat Mughshin in northern DHUFAR or al-Ramlah al-Hamrah, which lies between the DHAHIRAH province of OMAN and the great RUB' al-KHALI desert. The Rub' al-Khali itself is generally referred to by the badu (nomadic) tribes inhabiting it as al-Rimal.

RA'S al-HADD. The extreme eastern point of OMAN, as well as of the entire Arabian Peninsula. The point ends in a sandy beach marking the division between the Gulf of OMAN and the Arabian Sea.

RA'S al-KHAYMAH. One of the seven member states of the UNITED ARAB EMIRATES (UAE). Like SHARJAH, Ra's al-Khaymah was one of the major settlements of the QASIMI tribe which dominated the TRUCIAL COAST in the last several centuries. The coastal town and capital of the same name is one of the oldest ports in the Gulf and was long known as JULFAR. The area of the state is 600 square miles and the estimated population in the mid-1970s was 57, 282.

The major settlement is Ra's al-Khaymah Town, built around an estuary, where roughly a third of the population resides. Other settlements include Rams, Khatt and DIQDAQAH, one of the most important agricultural centers in the UAE.

al-RASASI see ISMA'IL BIN KHALIL al-RASASI

RASHID BIN HUMAYD al-NU'AYMI. Ruler of the State of 'AJMAN since 1928, he is the longest-serving ruler in the UNITED ARAB EMIRATES, as well as being the paramount shaykh of the NA'IM tribe. Although 'Ajman is the smallest of the UAE member states, Shaykh Rashid in the mid-1970s was highly respected in UAE councils, through the combination of his longevity, striking physical stature and personal courage.

RASHID BIN SA'ID AL MAKTUM. Ruler of DUBAY (r. 1958-) and Vice-President of the UNITED ARAB EMIRATES (UAE) since its inception in 1971. Shaykh Rashid is credited with having established Dubay as the preeminent commercial center and entrepôt of Eastern Arabia. Because of his business acumen, Dubay became relatively prosperous long before the discovery of oil in 1966. Revenues from petroleum, however, have added considerably to the financial base and made possible a number of major infrastructural schemes that in the late 1960s and early 1970s included a modern international harbor and airport and the most extensive dry-docking facilities between Rotterdam and Singapore. Shaykh Rashid personally led the party that took DAYRAH (on the other side of the estuary from Dubay Town) in the late 1940s from the control of a collateral line of the Al Maktum dynasty and reunited the state under the rule of Rashid's father, Shaykh Sa'id bin Maktum.

"RED" LINE. With the rapid expansion of the Kingdom of SAUDI ARABIA since the "BLUE" LINE of 1913 established the eastern boundary of NAJD (then part of the Ottoman Empire and later the territorial basis of the Saudi state), King 'Abd al-'Aziz bin 'Abd al-Rahman (commonly known as Ibn Sa'ud) presented to the British on April 3, 1935, a border claim (the "Red" Line) that ran considerably to the east of the former boundary. The "Red" Line would have placed the base of the QATAR Peninsula, KHAWR al-'UDAYD, the edges of al-DHAFRAH, and nearly all of the RUB' al-KHALI desert in Saudi territory. Negotiations concerning this boundary were held in London and al-Riyadh throughout 1935; in the same year the British proposed a modification of the Saudi claim that became known as the

REFORMED CHURCH see ARABIAN MISSION

RIBBING, HERBERT DE. Swedish Ambassador to Spain and Special Representative of the Secretary-General of the United Nations appointed to report on the "Question of Oman" before the U. N. regarding the alleged aggression against the IMAMATE of interior OMAN. De Ribbing visited Oman in May and June of 1963 and presented his report in October of the same year. His report concluded that the allegations were unfounded and that, in fact, the Imamate no longer existed in the interior. The report failed to satisfy the Arab members of the U. N. and two years later another U. N. Committee was formed to study the situation. This group was refused entry to Oman. Its report (the "Jiménez Report"), issued in 1965, called for self-determination in Oman and was generally unfavorable to the Sultanate, a view that was seconded by a majority of the members of the General Assembly in a vote that session.

RIFA' al-GHARBI. A settlement on al-BAHRAYN Island, located halfway between al-MANAMAH and al-'AWALI, it has been the residence of the Ruler of al-Bahrayn since the early 1940s and the daily majlis (audience) is held at the palace there.

al-RIMAL see al-RUB' al-KHALI

RIYADH LINE. A proposed boundary line between SAUDI ARABIA and the British-protected states of the Arabian Gulf, presented by the British to Saudi Arabia on November 25, 1935. The Riyadh Line was essentially a modification of the Saudi "RED" LINE presented earlier in 1935, which advanced the Saudi border a considerable distance eastward of the earlier de facto frontier established by the 1913 "BLUE" LINE. Although the Riyadh Line represented British willingness to concede much of the additional territory the Saudis claimed, it would have prevented Saudi ownership of the base of the QATAR Peninsula and the strategic KHAWR al-'UDAYD. This British "presentation" was academic as Saudi Arabia immediately rejected it. A boundary conference held in al-DAMMAM (Saudi Arabia) early in 1952 was equally unsuccessful and the problem continued to fester until Saudi Arabia announced even more expansive boundaries in August 1952 and backed them up with an armed occupation of al-BURAYMI oasis.

RIYAL [rial] (plural: riyalat). Traditional unit of currency derived from European coins of the 16th and 17th centuries (the word riyal comes from the Spanish real de plata). The unit is used in OMAN (1 riyal equals 1000 baizas), SAUDI ARABIA (1 riyal equals 100 halalahs) and QATAR (1 riyal equals 100 dirhams). The riyal Sa'idi (later riyal Omani) was introduced in Oman in 1970, replacing the Indian rupee (used on the coast) and the MARIA THERESA THALER (used in the interior).

RIYAM, BANI (singular: Riyami). One of the more important tribes of OMAN province and the JABAL al-AKHDAR in the Sultanate of OMAN. The Bani Riyam are IBADI in religion and for the last century have dominated the GHAFIRI political faction in the Sultanate. Major settlements include Mutti, Birkat al-Mawz, Manah, NIZWA, IZKI, SAYQ and Sharayjah (the last two being on the Jabal al-Akhdar). TANUF, the tribe's traditional headquarters, was destroyed by the order of Sultan SA'ID BIN TAYMUR AL BU SA'ID in 1957. Major sections include the Awlad Rashid, Al NABAHINAH, Awlad Riqaysh, Awlad Thani, Bani Tawbah and Sharayjiyyin. Although the Bani Riyam were originally a loose confederation of tribes, leadership of the whole has been provided for nearly two centuries by the Al Nabahinah. The most recent tamimah (paramount shaykh) was SULAYMAN BIN HIMYAR al-NABHANI, who fled to Saudi Arabia after the failure of the OMAN REVOLUTIONARY MOVEMENT (ORM) in 1959. Since then the tribe has been virtually leaderless and has lost much of its importance: because of its role in the 1950s revolt, it was discriminated against by Sultan Sa'id bin Taymur. The Bani RUWAHAH are the tribe's traditional adversaries, while the Bani Riyam have in the past enjoyed a special (almost client) relationship with the JANABAH badu tribe.

ROSS, EDWARD C. A 19th-century Government of India official in the Gulf who served briefly as Assistant Political Agent at the Sultanate of OMAN's enclave at GWADAR and later as Political Agent at MUSCAT from 1871 to 1872. In 1872, he succeeded Lewis PELLY as POLITICAL RESIDENT IN THE PERSIAN GULF (PRPG), in which post he remained until 1892. Unlike Pelly, who actively sought to "civilize" the area, Ross was content merely to strengthen British control. He was responsible for making the Residency directly responsible to Delhi, rather than to Bombay as was the case under Pelly, he strengthened measures against slave trading, curbed Ottoman influence in the Gulf, regularized British relations with the emirates under a protected-state system (during the period 1887-1892), and extended British influence in the Sultanate of Oman. Ross also established a reputation as a scholar and writer on the area, his best-known work being the "Annals of Oman," a translation of the Kashf al-Ghummah, a classical Arabic history.

al-RUB' al-KHALI. An Arabic phrase meaning the Empty Quarter, it is the largest desert of Arabia and one of the largest in the world. Cut off from moisture-bearing winds, it is composed largely of sand dunes punctuated infrequently by waterholes. Habitation is extremely sparse, consisting only of a few small badu (nomadic) tribes such as the 'AWAMIR, Rawashid, MANASIR, Sa'ar, Dawasir, Murrah and DURU', who generally refer to it simply as al-Rimal (the Sands). The first European to cross it was Bertram THOMAS (from SALALAH to QATAR) in 1929-1930; Thomas was closely followed by H. St. John B. PHILBY (from the Saudi or northern side). The explorer best acquainted with it, however, remains Wilfred THESIGER. The Rub' al-Khali long made for undemarcated frontiers for SAUDI ARABIA, ABU DHABI, the Sultanate of OMAN, the People's Democratic Republic of Yemen (PDRY; the successor to Aden Colony and Protectorate) and the Yemen Arab Republic (northern Yemen), but the potentiality for oil deposits beneath the sands has led to a greater interest among the leaders of these states in establishing definite and agreed upon boundaries.

al-RUSTAQ. The largest town of the HAJAR Mountains, it is the northern gateway to al-JABAL al-AKHDAR. It served as the capital of the YA'ARIBAH dynasty of OMANI IMAMS and for the Al Bu SA'ID dynasty during the latter half of the 18th century. The founder of the latter dynasty, AHMAD BIN SA'ID, is buried in al-Rustaq. The town remained semi-independent in the hands of a collateral branch of the Al Bu Sa'id until 1917 when it was captured by the Imamate. Al-Rustaq was not incorporated into the Sultanate until after the Imam's wali (governor), TALIB BIN 'ALI al-HINA'I, fled the area in 1955. The settlement is inhabited by sections of the 'IBRIYYIN, Bani GHAFIR and Bani KHARUS, and is dominated by a great stone fort that was built by the Ya'aribah on earlier foundations.

RU'US al-JIBAL. The precipitous mountain range which extends from the Western HAJAR Range to the end of the MUSANDAM PENINSULA. Due to its extreme ruggedness, the area has few inhabitants. Moreover, since the mountains come right down to the sea, there are few ports. The inhabitants are largely from the SHIHUH tribe, whose primary language is non-Arabic and who have traditionally been one of the most xenophobic tribes of Eastern Arabia. Political jurisdiction is split between the Sultanate of OMAN in the north, and the states of RA'S al-KHAYMAH, SHARJAH and al-FUJAYRAH (all three being members of the UNITED ARAB EMIRATES) as well as the main territory belonging to the Sultanate of Oman in the south. The major towns are KHASAB, DIBBA, al-Fujayrah, Lima and Bukha.

RUWAHAH, BANI (singular: Ruwahi). One of the largest tribes of OMAN, the Bani Ruwahah inhabit the area of the Wadi Bani Ruwahah, which is a continuation of the upper WADI SAMA'IL and the adjacent valleys of al-JABAL al-AKHDAR. They are IBADI, belong to the HINAWI political faction, and have the Bani RIYAM as their traditional adversaries. The major towns of the tribe are Upper Sama'il, al-Khudrah, Upper Qarut, and parts of IZKI. The tribe's weak position over the last century has been due to a lack of effective leadership. In a move to counter this deficiency, the leadership of the tribe was offered several generations ago to the KHALILI clan of the Bani KHARUS, who have remained the Ruwahi tamimahs (paramount shaykhs). One of them, MUHAMMAD BIN 'ABD ALLAH al-KHALILI, was IMAM from 1920 to 1954.

RUWI. A village of OMAN located in the Wadi Bayt al-Falaj, three miles southwest of MATRAH. Traditionally, it marked the entrance to the interior and until 1970, a gatehouse there collected taxes from caravans entering the MUSCAT/MATRAH area. Since the coup d'état of 1970, Ruwi has become the center of new housing complexes for government employees and a number of new retail businesses.

- S -

SAF see SULTAN'S ARMED FORCES

SABKHAH (plural: sibakh). Arabic term for salt marsh. Usually located in low areas next to the seacoast, it consists of a thin layer of hard-packed sand covering a slushy mixture of sand and salt water. Sabkhahs are extremely treacherous to men, vehicles and animals. They exist at many points along the southern coast of the GULF.

SABKHAT MATTI. An extensive salt marsh lying along the GULF coast in the extreme western part of the State of ABU DHABI. It extends along the coast for approximately 30 miles and to the east it flanks al-DHAFRAH region for some 60 miles inland until it merges with the RUB' al-KHALI desert.

SA'D, YAL (singular: Yal Sa'di). One of the largest tribes of OMAN, settled principally along the BATINAH Coast in the vicinity of al-SUWAYQ and al-MASNA-'AH, although some groups extend into the Western HAJAR. It is IBADI and GHAFIRI. Possibly because of the vulnerability of their territory on the Batinah, they have remained remarkably neutral in tribal politics and thus possess no special adversaries or allies.

SA'DIYAT ISLAND. Situated only a short distance from ABU DHABI Island, Sa'diyat is the location of an Arid Lands Research Center begun by the University of Arizona. The heart of the project is five acres of greenhouse agriculture utilizing techniques similar to that of hydroponics, as well as distillation of seawater, controlled temperature and humidity, and feeding. The Center was producing an impressive average of five tons of produce (tomatos, cucumbers, etc.) per year in the mid-1970s.

SAHAM. A settlement on the northern BATINAH Coast, under the sovereignty of the Sultanate of OMAN, and approximately 15 miles southeast of SUHAR. In the 19th and early 20th centuries, it formed part of the territories ruled by the semi-independent Al Bu SA'ID walis (governors) of Suhar.

SA'ID, AL BU (singular: Al Bu Sa'idi). An Omani tribe of al-SHARQIYYAH and OMAN provinces, centered around the towns of ADAM, NIZWA, Manah and IZKI (and from which some members emigrated to East Africa in the 19th and early 20th centuries). A family from this tribe has provided the ruling dynasty of Oman since 1744, when AHMAD BIN SA'ID, the wali (governor) of SUHAR, drove the Persian invaders out of Oman and was subsequently elected Imam. The Al Bu Sa'id moved the capital of Oman from the interior (then at al-RUSTAQ) to MUSCAT, which resulted in the loss of the title of Imam and the eventual adoption of the title of SULTAN. This move also turned the attention of Oman's rulers towards the sea and lands beyond (the dynasty at one time or another ruled ZANZIBAR, much of the East African coast, part of the Makran coast of what is now Pakistan, HORMUZ and Bandar 'Abbas in what is now Iran, and al-BAHRAYN). But this outward expansion entailed a loss of control over the interior of Oman and a split between the coastal Sultanate (based on MUSCAT/MATRAH) and a semi-autonomous interior (where tribal rulers predominated and an Imam resided at NIZWA at intermittent intervals), a situation which lasted until 1955. Since the coup d'état of July 23, 1970, the head of the family (as well as tamimah or paramount shaykh of the tribe) has been Sultan QABUS BIN SA'ID. A number of close relations of Qabus hold important positions in the Sultanate's government and more distant relatives have traditionally provided the bulk of the walis. The tribe (and ruling family) is IBADI. Although the tribe is Hinawi, the ruling family has placed itself above the GHAFIRI-HINAWI political dichotomy by pursuing a changing pattern of tribal alliances on both sides and by relying on outside (primarily British) assistance. Other important Sultans from the same family have been SA'ID BIN SULTAN (r. 1807-1856), FAYSAL BIN TURKI (r. 1888-1913), TAYMUR BIN FAYSAL (r. 1913-1931), SA'ID BIN TAYMUR (r. 1932-1970) and QABUS BIN SA'ID (r. 1970-). Imam 'AZZAN BIN QAYS (r. 1868-1871) was from a collateral line of the Al Bu Sa'id.

SA'ID BIN KHALFAN al-KHALILI. OMANI religious leader of the mid-19th century. In 1868, he joined forces with the IMAM, 'AZZAN BIN QAYS AL BU SA'ID, and became 'Azzan's principal adviser during the three years that the Imam held MUSCAT. He was killed along with his son Ahmad in 1871 when Turki bin Sa'id Al Bu Sa'id captured Muscat and restored the Sultanate. His grandson, MUHAMMAD BIN 'ABD ALLAH al-KHALILI, was elected Imam in 1913.

SA'ID BIN SULTAN AL BU SA'ID. Known as Sa'id the Great, he became Sultan of OMAN (r. 1807-1856) after assassinating his cousin, Badr bin Sayf (r. 1804-1806). In order to consolidate his hold over the country he was forced to withstand repeated SAUDI challenges (backed by Egypt) and increasing disenchantment by interior tribes. But by 1820, he was strong enough to consider expansion: DHUFAR was loosely annexed in 1829, several campaigns were led against al-BAHRAYN in the 1820s and increasing territory was captured along the East African littoral beginning in 1832. Eventually Sa'id moved his capital to the island of ZANZIBAR and lived there permanently, returning to Oman only periodically. His reign was marked by cooperation with the Europeans and expansion of trade and commercial ties. These, in turn, led to treaties with the United States (1833)--the first Arab emissary to the U. S. (in 1840) was an Omani; France (1844); and the Netherlands (1877), as well as Great Britain. On his death in 1856, Zanzibar and Oman were divided between two of his 20 sons and in 1861, the CANNING AWARD ratified this permanent division of the Al Bu Sa'id empire.

SA'ID BIN TAYMUR AL BU SA'ID. Succeeded his father, TAYMUR BIN FAYSAL, as Sultan of OMAN in 1932 and was deposed by his son, QABUS BIN SA'ID, in July 1970. Educated in India and Baghdad, Sa'id returned to MUSCAT in 1929 to become President of the Sultanate's Council of Ministers, a post giving him effective control of the state during his father's frequent absence. After becoming Sultan in February 1932, he set to work to restore some measure of the independence enjoyed by his illustrious namesake, SA'ID BIN SULTAN (r. 1807-1856). In the mid-1940s, Sa'id entered into correspondence with the major tribal leaders of the Oman interior in hopes of supplanting the IMAM, MUHAMMAD BIN 'ABD ALLAH al-KHALILI, on the latter's death, but these plans were never put into action, as GHALIB BIN 'ALI al-HINA'I was elected Muhammad's successor when the Imam finally died in 1954. After more than a year of preparation, Sa'id personally accompanied his military forces into the interior in December 1955, thus formally reuniting Oman for the first time since the turn of the century. However, a revolt led by the OMAN REVOLUTIONARY MOVEMENT (ORM) broke out in 1957, having been backed by SAUDI ARABIA and Arab nationalist forces, and was extinguished only by a combined Sultanate-British offensive on the JABAL al-AKHDAR mountain in January 1959. Always aloof from his people, Sa'id retreated to the southern town of SALALAH in mid-1958 and never returned to the capital, preferring to conduct state business by wireless to the handful of Arab, Indian and British officials in Muscat. Sa'id's cautious attitude towards development once he began receiving oil revenues, combined with his refusal to allow Oman to escape its medieval character and the growing success of radical rebels in DHUFAR (who unsuccessfully tried to assassinate him in 1966), eventually caused his son to organize a coup d'état against him. Sa'id was wounded when elements of the SULTAN'S ARMED FORCES stormed Salalah Palace on the night of July 23, 1970, and was taken by RAF plane to al-BAHRAYN and then on to London, where he lived until his death in October 1972.

SALALAH. The capital of the southern Omani province of DHUFAR and, with an estimated 25,000 to 35,000 inhabitants, one of the largest towns in the Sultanate of OMAN. The town has one of the most favorable climates in the Arabian Peninsula as it is the only part touched by the Indian Ocean monsoon (June-September), which reduces the summer heat and turns the city green. Salalah was conquered by the Al Bu SA'ID dynasty of Oman in the early 19th century, but effective control was not exercised until the 1890s. In the 1920s, Sultan TAYMUR BIN FAYSAL spent much of his time there, a practice that was followed by his son SA'ID. Eventually Sa'id made Salalah Palace his permanent home and never returned to MUSCAT. The present Sultan, QABUS BIN SA'ID, who was born and grew up in Salalah, was placed under virtual house arrest there after his return to Oman from schooling in 1966 until the coup d'état in 1970. The town, consisting of several distinct settlements (including old Salalah, al-Husn, al-Rabat, and al-Balid), is located midway along the coast of Salalah Plain which is about 30 miles long and is at its widest point approximately 10 miles across. Since its beach on the Indian Ocean exhibits a heavy surf, a new port has been built a few miles to the west at Raysut. The inhabitants of Salalah are predominantly Arab (from the KATHIR tribe, especially the Ruwwas, Marhun and Shanafir sections), and Negro (descendents of slaves brought from Africa), with some QARA. At the height of the DHUFAR REBELLION,

Salalah was sealed off from the rebels by a barbed wire perimeter fence. Even so, the nearby (British) Royal Air Force Base became a frequent target of rocket attacks. The town's rapid growth after 1970 was a function of its being opened to Dhufari tribesmen and of the priority given it by the Sultanate's vastly expanded development program.

SALAMAH WA-BINATUHA [The Quoins]. In English, "Salamah and her daughters." This is a group of three small islands approximately five to seven miles north of Musandam Island in the Strait of HORMUZ. They mark the entrance to the Arabian Gulf from the Gulf of OMAN and the main shipping channel lies between them and Musandam Island, rather than between them and the Iranian island of Qishm (which is a much wider distance).

SALIH BIN 'ALI al-HARITHI. Tamimah (paramount shaykh) of the HIRTH tribe of al-SHARQIYYAH province of eastern OMAN and head of the HINAWI tribal confederation during the latter half of the 19th century. He first gained attention in 1859 for his attempts, in league with Thuwayni bin Sa'id Al Bu Sa'id, the Ruler of Oman, to supplant the Sultan of ZANZIBAR, Thuwayni's brother Majid. When the attempt failed, he returned to Oman and forged an alliance with SA'ID BIN KHALFAN al-KHALILI and 'AZZAN BIN QAYS AL BU SA'ID. When 'Azzan was proclaimed IMAM and captured MUSCAT in 1868 from the main branch of the AL BU SA'ID, Salih served as one of his major advisers until 'Azzan was killed in 1871 and the movement dissipated. Salih thereupon conducted periodic campaigns throughout the remainder of the century aimed at regaining control of Muscat; these campaigns largely remained unsuccessful because of his inability to attract the GHAFIRI faction to his side. He managed to occupy MATRAH in 1874 and 1877, then laid siege to Muscat in 1883 before finally capturing the town (but not the forts overlooking it) in 1895. After two months of stalemate, Sultan FAYSAL BIN TURKI persuaded the rebels to withdraw. Salih died of wounds after a skirmish in the Sharqiyyah in the following year and was succeeded as tamimah by his son, 'ISA BIN SALIH.

SALIH BIN 'ISA al-HARITHI. Tamimah (paramount shaykh) of the HIRTH tribe of al-SHARQIYYAH province in eastern OMAN and leader of the HINAWI tribal confederation. Salih succeeded his brother Muhammad as tamimah of the Hirth (Muhammad had been tamimah only several years after the death of 'ISA BIN SALIH) after overcoming a challenge from Muhammad's son AHMAD. Salih supported the IMAMATE of GHALIB BIN 'ALI al-HINA'I and when the Imamate fell in December 1955, Salih fled the country, later representing the Imamate in Cairo as "Prince of the Sharqiyyah" and "Deputy Imam." He broke with the other leaders of the ex-Imamate in 1961 and thereafter lived in Egypt.

SALIM BIN RASHID al-KHARUSI (d. 1920). Elected IBADI IMAM of OMAN in 1913 as a protégé of Himyar bin Nasir al-Nabhani and 'ABD ALLAH BIN HUMAYD al-SALIMI. As the first Imam since 'AZZAN BIN QAYS AL BU SA'ID (d. 1871), he served as the focal point for a seven-year revolt against the Sultanate of OMAN which finally resulted in the Agreement of al-SIB (1920). He was assassinated in the WADI 'ANDAM several months before the Agreement was signed. His son, 'Abd Allah bin Salim, was an unsuccessful candidate for Imam in the election of 1954.

al-SALIMI see 'ABD ALLAH BIN HUMAYD al-SALIMI

SALMAN BIN HAMAD AL KHALIFAH. Ruler of al-BAHRAYN from 1942 to 1961 whose reign was marked by a number of governmental and economic improvements. A renegotiation of the oil concession terms with the BAHRAIN PETROLEUM CO. (BAPCO) in the early 1950s provided the means for improving and expanding al-BAHRAYN's economic infrastructure, including the construction of Mina' Salman (Port Salman). Shaykh Salman's visit to SAUDI ARABIA in 1958 resulted in a demarcation of al-Bahrayni and Saudi Arabian territorial waters. The Bahrayn Labor Law, the first and only one of its kind in the Lower Gulf, was promulgated during Salman's reign, which also witnessed the relinquishment of certain extraterritorial rights by the British. The latter years of his rule were marked by considerable political unrest, one consequence of which (in addition to the Labor Law) was the introduction of partially elected municipal councils as well as councils responsible for health and educational affairs. He was succeeded by his son, 'ISA BIN SALMAN.

SAMA'IL see WADI SAMA'IL

SAMHAN see JABAL SAMHAN

SAQR BIN MUHAMMAD al-QASIMI. Ruler of RA'S al-KHAYMAH (r. 1948-) and member of the Supreme Council of Rulers of the UNITED ARAB EMIRATES (UAE) since 1972. Shaykh Saqr came to power in a government takeover that ousted Shaykh Sultan bin Salim al-Qasimi (r. 1921-1948) from the rulership. One of the stronger personalities among the seven heads of state in the UAA, his politics have often been controversial. Unlike his late cousin, former Ruler of SHARJAH Shaykh KHALID BIN MUHAMMAD al-QASIMI, he refused to cooperate with IRAN over the TUNB ISLANDS (Greater and Lesser Tunbs) dispute in late 1971. As a result, these islands were forcibly wrested from his control by an Iranian naval expedition. This act, which cost the lives of a number of Ra's al-Khaymah citizens who resisted the Iranian invasion, was roundly condemned in most quarters of the Arab world. For his part in ordering the local defence force to resist the occupation, and for his subsequent leadership of street demonstrations called to protest the incident, he emerged from the episode as a kind of folk hero in the eyes of his subjects and to many others in the Arab world.

SAQR BIN SULTAN al-QASIMI. The Ruler of the State of SHARJAH from 1951 to 1965. Throughout much of his reign Shaykh Saqr criticized British policy in the region. During the 1960s, he demonstrated a close affinity with Egyptian President Nasser. In reaction to Saqr's promise to a pro-Nasser representative of the Arab League to do all within his power to facilitate the establishment of an Arab League office in his emirate, British officials in Sharjah, with the aid of members of the Qasimi ruling family, arranged a coup d'état in 1965 which resulted in Saqr's replacement by his cousin, KHALID BIN MUHAMMAD. Saqr subsequently went into exile in Egypt until early 1972, when he returned to Sharjah and attempted to stage another coup d'état and regain the rulership. This attempt was frustrated by the prompt action of units of the Sharjan and United Arab Emirates' defense forces, and Saqr was captured. Khalid was killed in this coup attempt and succeeded by his brother, SULTAN BIN MUHAMMAD. As of the mid-1970s, Shaykh Saqr was still imprisoned in ABU DHABI. The initiation of formal trial proceedings against him had been postponed indefinitely because of a fear of possible negative political repercussions.

SA'UD BIN JILUWI. A mid-20th-century governor of al-Hasa province of SAUDI ARABIA who was in charge of the Saudi occupation of al-BURAYMI oasis in 1952. Thereafter he continued to direct operations in that area from al-Hasa until the TRUCIAL OMAN SCOUTS forced the Saudi garrison to withdraw in 1955. For a period in 1955, Sa'ud's son, 'Abd al-'Aziz, acted as governor of al-Hasa in his father's place.

SAUDI ARABIA AND EASTERN ARABIA. With the religious impetus given them in the mid-18th century by the appearance of the MUWAHHIDUN or Wahhabis (more correctly called Unitarians, a fundamentalist school of SUNNI Islam), the Saudi dynasty of the NAJD of central Arabia embarked on a program of expansion that eventually swept across much of Arabia and left its mark on Eastern Arabia. By 1800, the Saudis had established a garrison at the strategic oasis of al-BURAYMI, a gateway to Eastern Arabia and this was subsequently used as an advance base for further incursions into the area (although Saudi sovereignty over the oasis was never firmly established).

In 1803, a Saudi expedition to the BATINAH Coast on the Gulf of OMAN sacked the town of al-SUWAYQ and successfully staged a siege on SUHAR. Only with the payment of ZAKAT (used by the Saudis as a type of tribute but paid by the OMANI Sultans as a form of protection) did they withdraw. By 1807, the Saudis had established a garrison further north at KHAWR FAKKAN in league with the QASIMI shaykh of RA'S al-KHAYMAH, and three years later they beat back a joint Anglo-Omani expedition against the town of SHINAS, which the Saudi-Qasimi forces had captured. The latter coalition even drove the Omanis back down the coast to MUSCAT, capturing NAKHL and SAMA'IL on the way. In 1812, the Omanis asked for and received help from the Persians. The aid received proved ineffective, as the joint Omani-Persian army was nearly annihilated near IZKI. The next year the Saudis plundered MATRAH and cut a path through JA'LAN (southeastern Oman) with the help of the Bani Bu 'ALI tribe. The withdrawal of the invaders in 1814 followed the death that year of the Saudi commander, MUTLAQ al-MUTAYRI, and the death of the Saudi Emir in Dara'iyah (the Saudi capital). The Egyptian sacking of Dara'iyah in 1818 and the destruction of Ra's al-Khaymah by the British in 1819 provided a decade of respite for Eastern Arabia. However, the Saudi threat was resurrected in 1830 and was appeased only by annual payment of zakat.

Al-Buraymi was recaptured in 1845, and once again only zakat eased the spectre of invasion on the Batinah, as did similar payments in 1853. In 1864, an alliance between the Saudis and 'AZZAN BIN QAYS AL BU SA'ID was instrumental in boosting his bid for control of Oman but once he captured Muscat he turned foe. 'Azzan's forces captured al-Buraymi from the Saudis in 1869, the last time they were to see the oasis until the mid-20th century.

With the revival of Saudi fortunes after the recapture of the new capital at al-Riyadh by 'Abd al-'Aziz bin 'Abd al-Rahman Al Sa'ud (more commonly known as Ibn Sa'ud) in 1902, the foundations of the modern Saudi Kingdom took root, and throughout the early to mid-20th century, Saudi Arabia expanded in all directions possible. A Saudi military detachment occupied al-Buraymi oasis in August of 1952 against the objections of the State of ABU DHABI and the Sultanate of OMAN (which were supported by Britain). A deadlock in the subsequent arbitration led to the explusion of the Saudi garrison in October 1955 by the TRUCIAL OMAN SCOUTS. Saudi acquiescence in the de facto border settlement was not achieved, however, until August 1974, when boundary agreements were reached with Abu Dhabi regarding al-Buraymi, the Zararrah (Sha'iba) oil fields, and KHAWR al-'UDAYD. Traditional Saudi estrangement from the Sultanate was ameliorated during the course of a visit to al-Riyadh by Sultan QABUS BIN SA'ID AL BU SA'ID in December 1971. The above-mentioned boundary agreement also paved the way for Saudi Arabia to establish diplomatic relations with the UNITED ARAB EMIRATES. Relations with QATAR have always been warm and this has also been true of 20th-century Saudi relations with al-BAHRAYN (by the second half of the century, the Bahrayn oil refinery was heavily dependent on Saudi oil brought by undersea pipeline from the mainland).

SAYQ. A settlement located on a plateau on the JABAL al-AKHDAR massif in central OMAN. The village is inhabited by the Bani RIYAM tribe and was headquarters for the leaders of the OMAN REVOLUTIONARY MOVEMENT (ORM) from 1957 to 1959. After it was captured by a joint Sultanate of OMAN-British military force in 1959, a military camp of the SULTAN's ARMED FORCES and an airstrip were built there and a training mission was established in the mid-1970s. Along with the neighboring settlements of Shurayjah and Wadi Bani Habib, Sayq is the site of some of the most intensive cultivation in Oman, utilizing steep mountainside terracing to grow a number of different crops.

SAYYID (plural: sadat). An Arabic term originally defined to mean the descendants of al-Husayn, a grandson of the Prophet Muhammad. In OMAN, the Al Bu SA'ID rulers became known as sayyids after dropping the title of IMAM in 1784. Later the British introduced the title of SULTAN (which was eventually accepted by the populace as well), and the term sayyid was thereafter reserved for use by members of the ruling family. In addition, there is a small group of sayyids (in the original sense of the word) who reside in the DHUFAR province of southern Oman. The term has also come to be used as a prefix to the name of an adult male; in such cases the meaning is equivalent to "mister" in English.

SHAFI'I see SHARI'AH

SHAKHBUT BIN SULTAN AL NUHAYYAN. Ruler of the State of ABU DHABI from 1928 to 1966. His long reign contrasted strongly with that of his immediate predecessors, several of whom died violently at one another's hands. Shakhbut's downfall was due primarily to his inability to deal effectively with the huge influx of oil wealth after 1962, and he was deposed in a bloodless coup d'état in 1966 in favor of his younger brother, Shaykh ZAYID BIN SULTAN. Shakhbut thereafter lived for a brief period in Iran and then retired to al-'AYN oasis in Abu Dhabi.

SHAMIS, AL BU (singular: Shamsi). Tribe of al-BURAYMI area of OMAN. Originally part of the NA'IM tribe, they have long been at odds with the rest of the tribe. They inhabit al-Hamasah village in al-Buraymi oasis and a badu (nomadic) section is centered around DANK in al-DHAHIRAH province of the Sultanate of OMAN. The Al Bu Shamis are SUNNI in religion and GHAFIRI in politics (although the group around Dank is HINAWI).

SHARI'AH. The body of Islamic law which governs many aspects of life in Eastern Arabia. Although based on the Koran [Qur'an] and the sunnah (the example set by the Prophet Muhammad in his deeds and sayings, or hadiths), various interpretations of the shari'ah rely upon the individual judgment (ra'y) of the judge (QADI), analogy (qiyas), and/or consensus (ijma') of the theological community. These differing interpretations have been consolidated into four schools of Islamic jurisprudence: the Hanafi, Hanbali, Maliki and Shafi'i. A Muslim may belong to whichever school he chooses and have legal action concerning him conducted by a qadi of that school. Among the SUNNIS of Eastern Arabia (Sunnism being the main body of ISLAM; other sects do not follow the above four schools of jurisprudence), the majority follow the Shafi'i interpretation. Some, however, belong to the Maliki (e.g., the ruling families of al-BAHRAYN and ABU DHABI) and others to the Hanbali (e.g., the dynasties of 'AJMAN, QATAR, RA'S al-KHAYMAH, SHARJAH and UMM al-QAYWAYN and the MUWAHHIDUN or Wahhabis of SAUDI ARABIA).

SHARJAH [al-Shariqah]. One of the seven member states of the UNITED ARAB EMIRATES (UAE). Sharjah has had a long and eventful history, being one of the most important centers of the Qasimi tribe, which has dominated the UAE coast in the past: at one time, the states of RA'S al-KHAYMAH and al-FUJAYRAH were subservient to it. Sharjah was the headquarters of the British Political Agent for the TRUCIAL COAST until 1955 when the Agency was moved to neighboring DUBAY. It was also the site of a British Royal Air Force (RAF) station from 1940 (which was also the first airport in the region). The TRUCIAL OMAN SCOUTS (TOS) were later established there (it is still the headquarters of the UAE Defence Force, successor to the TOS) and British troops were stationed there until the official British withdrawal in 1971.

The area of the state is approximately 1000 square miles and the estimated population in the mid-1970s was between 85,000 and 90,000. The seat of government and main settlement is Sharjah Town, located astride an estuary and serving as residence for approximately two-thirds of the State's population. Other settlements include al-DHAYD (inland), and KALBAH, KHAWR FAKKAN and part of DIBBA, all of which are on the Gulf of OMAN. Principal islands are Sir Abu Nu'ayr and ABU MUSA (under partial Iranian occupation since 1971). The major tribe is the QAWASIM but there are also members of the Bani QITAB and numerous other tribes. The most renowned of its Rulers was SULTAN BIN SAQR al-QASIMI, who reigned from ca. 1803 to 1866. More recent Rulers have been

SAQR BIN SULTAN (r. 1951-1965), KHALID BIN MUHAMMAD (r. 1965-1972), and SULTAN BIN MUHAMMAD (since 1972). Sharjah joined the ranks of the oil producing countries in 1974.

al-SHARQIYYAH. Geographical province of the eastern interior of OMAN. It is bounded on the north by the Eastern HAJAR Mountains, on the east by JA'LAN province, on the south by the WAHIBAH SANDS and on the west by OMAN province and the edges of the RUB' al-KHALI desert. The region as a whole is strongly IBADI and HINAWI in political orientation, the major tribes being the HIRTH, the Habus, the Masakirah, the Hajariyyin, the Al Bu SA'ID and the Yal WAHIBAH. The major settlements are Ibra, al-QABIL, al-Mintirib, al-Mudaybi, Samad, ADAM, and Bidiyyah. The Hirth tribe has long been the dominant power in the province and the last Harithi tamimah (paramount shaykh), AHMAD BIN MUHAMMAD, functioned as de facto ruler of the entire province in the 1950s and 1960s in the name of Sultan SA'ID BIN TAYMUR AL BU SA'ID.

al-SHARQIYYIN (singular: Sharqi). The predominant tribe of the state of al-FUJAYRAH. The tribe is SUNNI and GHAFIRI. The members were long dominated by the QASIMI tribe, but the British recognized their shaykh--MUHAMMAD BIN HAMAD AL SHARQI--as independent in 1952. At that time al-Fujayrah became one of the TRUCIAL STATES, and since 1971, a member of the UNITED ARAB EMIRATES.

SHAWIYAH (singular: Shawawi). An OMANI term referring to the nomads of mountains or in areas that are otherwise settled. They are typically goatherders.

SHAYKH [sheik] (plural: shuyukh). A title ordinarily given to the chief of a tribe. The term is also used as an honorific title for respected male elders, and as a title for Rulers (and other members of the dynasties) of the Arab states of the GULF, which are frequently referred to as "shaykhdoms" in much the same manner as states headed by kings are often referred to as kingdoms.

SHEIK see SHAYKH

SHIHAB al-DIN AHMAD BIN MAJID. A 15th-century Arab navigator of the Indian Ocean, most probably born at

RA'S al-KHAYMAH (then known as JULFAR) although the towns of SUR and SUHAR in OMAN also claim him. He served as navigator to Vasco da Gama on the first PORTUGUESE voyage across the Indian Ocean in 1498. Ahmad is also remembered for his maritime texts and nautical dictionaries covering the Indian Ocean, the Red Sea and the Arabian Gulf.

SHIHUH (singular: Shihuhi or Shihi). The mountain tribe inhabiting the RU'US al-JIBAL and MUSANDAM PENINSULA area of the Sultanate of OMAN. The tribe is noted for its primitive life style, history of extreme xenophobia and ethnic distinction from other tribes of Eastern Arabia. There are four components: al-Kumazarah (fishermen of the Musandam Peninsula who derive their name from the village of Kumzar; they speak what is believed to be an ancient mixture of Arabic and Persian); al-Dhuhuriyyin (apparently, remnants of a separate tribe assimilated into the Shihuh; they are fishermen centered around KHAWR al-SHAMM/ Elphinstone Inlet and GHUBBAT al-GHAZIRAH/Malcolm's Inlet); the Bani Hadiyyah and the Bani Shatayr (who are badu of the interior mountains or otherwise often live in caves). Only the Kumazarah speak a non-Arabic language as their primary tongue. Politically they are divided into two factions (the Bani Hadiyyah align with half of the Dhuhuriyin; and the Kumazarah with the Bani Shatayr and the remaining Dhuhuriyyin) although the tribe as a whole is strongly HINAWI--probably because of its long-standing feud with the neighboring QASIMI tribe, which is GHAFIRI. Although SUNNI, members of the tribe have long exhibited traces of animism.

SHI'I. A member of the Shi'ah sect of ISLAM, the largest surviving sect that broke away from the SUNNI (or orthodox) main body of Muslims. Shi'is believe that leadership of the Islamic community should have continued through the descendants of the Prophet Muhammad's grandsons. The Zaydi, or Fiver, subsect of Shi'ah holds that there were only five such leaders or IMAMs (the Zaydis are today confined to YEMEN). The Isma'ili, or Sevener, subsect believes that seven Imams existed (Isma'ilis were fairly numerous in the MUSCAT/MATRAH area of Oman prior to 1948 but have since resided primarily in the Indian subcontinent), while Ithna'ashari, or Twelver, Shi'is believe there were 12 Imams. Ithna'ashari Shi'ah is the state religion of IRAN and many Ithna'asharis are found in al-BAHRAYN, OMAN and elsewhere in Eastern Arabia.

SHINAS. A settlement along the northern BATINAH Coast under the sovereignty of the Sultanate of OMAN. It is located halfway between al-FUJAYRAH and SUHAR, and the inhabitants include BALUCHIS and members of the BANI KA'B and Riyayisah tribes. In the 19th and early 20th centuries, it formed part of the territories ruled by the semi-independent Al Bu SA'ID walis (governors) of Suhar. It was captured by a combined SAUDI-QAWASIM force in the first decade of the 19th century and recaptured after an intense battle by a combined British and Sultanate force.

al-SIB, AGREEMENT OF. Signed on September 25, 1920, between the tribal leaders of the OMAN interior on one hand, and the government of the Sultanate of OMAN on the other, through the mediation of the (British) Political Agent in MUSCAT, R. E. L. WINGATE, at the village of al-Sib on the BATINAH Coast (about 30 miles west of Muscat). The agreement marked the end of seven years of rebellion and the beginning of 35 years of peace. By its terms, the interior tribes pledged to: (1) live in peace with the Sultanate; (2) not restrict trade and travel with the coast; (3) return fugitives from justice, and (4) honor claims of coastal merchants. The Sultanate, in turn, agreed to: (1) not charge more than 5 per cent duty on exports from the interior to the coast; (2) guarantee interior tribesmen safety and freedom on the coast; (3) impose no restrictions on entry to and exit from coastal towns; (4) return fugitives from interior justice and not interfere with the tribes' internal affairs. With the IMAMATE issue and the OMAN REVOLUTIONARY MOVEMENT (ORM) of the 1950s, Arab nationalists used the Agreement to argue that an independent "Imamate of Oman" (as opposed to a "Sultanate of Muscat") had been created in the interior and that British actions in 1957 and 1959 were attempts to aid the Sultanate to conquer an independent country. These allegations were denied by the Sultan and the British, and although the attention of the United Nations was engaged for over a decade, the allegations were never generally accepted. Al-Sib is also the site of a modern international airport built in the early 1970s.

SIFALAH see 'ALAYAH-SIFALAH

SITRA ISLAND. A small island approximately five miles in length located off the eastern shore of al-BAHRAYN Island to which it is connected by a bridge. It is the site of an oil tank depot and wharf belonging to the BAHRAIN PETROLEUM CO. (BAPCO) and is also used as a resort by the inhabitants of al-MANAMAH. The island was the site of an attempted invasion by SA'ID BIN SULTAN AL BU SA'ID, the Sultan of OMAN, in 1828.

SLAVERY. Being a legal institution under the laws of ISLAM, the ownership and trading of slaves were practices engaged in for centuries by the inhabitants of the Arabian Peninsula and other parts of the Muslim world. The maritime prowess of the littoral peoples of Eastern Arabia enabled a prosperous slave trade to exist for many years between East Africa and Arabia as well as other nearby regions such as Baluchistan. The cessation of the trade was begun at the urging of the British who pressured the Arab states involved in the traffic (principally the Al Bu SA'ID Sultanate of OMAN) to restrict the activities of their vessels and, subsequently, to abolish the trade altogether. Nevertheless, the illegal importation of slaves continued until well into the 20th century, often through the port of SUR and frequently funneled into the Arabian hinterland through al-BURAYMI oasis. The most important spur to the decline of slavery, now illegal in every Arab state, has probably been the introduction of Western taboos against it.

SOHAR see SUHAR

SUDAN (singular: Suwaydi). A scattered tribe of Eastern Arabia found particularly in al-BAHRAYN, QATAR and the UNITED ARAB EMIRATES (UAE), especially the State of ABU DHABI. Its members are sometimes included as a section of the Bani YAS tribe, and are mainly HANBALI SUNNI Muslims. A member of this tribe, Ahmad Khalifah al-Suwaydi, the first university graduate of Abu Dhabi, was appointed to the post of Minister of Foreign Affairs in the first cabinet of the UAE in 1971.

SUHAR. A port and the largest settlement along the BATINAH Coast of OMAN. Its origins are prehistoric and, in the past, its inhabitants included Christians and Jews as well as Muslims; Islam was allegedly brought to Suhar during the lifetime of the Prophet Muhammad by 'Amr ibn al-'As. Suhar was a prosperous and well-known port of the medieval period (the great Muslim traveler Ibn Battutah spoke highly of it) until its decline following successive invasions by Persians and Portuguese. When Nadir Shah's troops invaded Oman in the 1730s to support a candidate for the IBADI IMAMATE, Suhar was the only town to resist them successfully. Its wali (governor), AHMAD BIN SA'ID AL BU SA'ID, first reached a truce with the Persians and then proceeded to drive them out of Oman, whereupon he was subsequently elected Imam himself. For the next two centuries, Suhar remained independent (or semi-independent) of the Al Bu Sa'id ruling household in MUSCAT, being governed by either a collateral branch of the Muscat dynasty or in virtual autonomy by a brother or uncle of the Sultan in Muscat. This situation came to an end only in 1930. Suhar is also important as a gateway to al-BURAYMI oasis via the WADI al-JIZZI.

SULAYMAN BIN HIMYAR al-NABHANI. Successor in 1920 to his father, Himyar bin Nasir, tamimah (paramount shaykh) of the Bani RIYAM tribe of the Sultanate of OMAN. Gradually through the years, he also acquired his father's political stature and was generally acknowledged as the head of the GHAFIRI tribal faction. He was the major supporter of Imam GHALIB BIN 'ALI al-HINA'I (r. 1954-1955). When Ghalib's brother, TALIB BIN 'ALI, returned from SAUDI ARABIA in 1957 with an army of the OMAN REVOLUTIONARY MOVEMENT (ORM), Sulayman led his tribe on the side of the rebels but was forced to retreat to his village of SAYQ on the JABAL al-AKHDAR and eventually (1959) into exile in Saudi Arabia. As a consequence, Sulayman lost the tamimahship of the Bani Riyam (they have not had one since) and his three ancestral homes (in TANUF, Birkat al-Mawz and Sayq) were destroyed by the British at the behest of then Sultan SA'ID BIN TAYMUR. Long noted for his political ambitions, Sulayman frequently referred to himself as "King of the Green Mountain."

SULTAN. Title applied to the Rulers of OMAN since the early 19th century. Initially, the term was used only by the British, the Rulers then being more commonly known by the title of SAYYID, but Sultan was generally accepted by the end of the century. Sultan is also a popular given name in Eastern Arabia.

SULTAN BIN MUHAMMAD al-QASIMI. Ruler of the State of SHARJAH since 1972. He is the only ruler among the emirates of Eastern Arabia with a university education (College of Agriculture, Cairo University). Prior to becoming Ruler, he was the UAE Minister for Education and Training. In 1973 he became the first UAE ruler to visit the United States and during that year he also served as chairman of the commission charged with recommending ways to reform the UAE governmental structure. His strong personal position in the mid-1970s was in contrast to that of his late brother, KHALID BIN MUHAMMAD, who was assassinated in an unsuccessful coup d'état in 1972. This was partly due to the fact that SHARJAH's social and economic position has improved with the abolition of British restrictions on the freedom of the Ruler, and with the production of oil since 1973. It also stemmed from Shaykh Sultan's close relationship with Shaykh ZAYID BIN SULTAN AL NUHAYYAN, the Ruler of Abu Dhabi and President of the UAE.

SULTAN BIN SAQR al-QASIMI. Shaykh of the QASIMI tribe and Ruler of SHARJAH from the early 19th century to 1866. Throughout his long career, relations with the British and his neighbors in OMAN and SAUDI ARABIA were frequently stormy. He was forced to recognize British supremacy on the sea in 1805 (and did so formally by the GENERAL TREATY of 1820). In 1808, he was deposed as the Ruler of RA'S al-KHAYMAH by the Saudis and taken to Dara'iyyah (the old Saudi capital in central Arabia). Returning to Sharjah in 1813, he became its Ruler with the help of the Omani Sultan and after the British destroyed Ra's al-Khaymah in a punitive expedition, Sultan bin Saqr was allowed to take charge there as well. Through close relatives, he thereafter ruled Sharjah, Ra's al-Khaymah, Hamriyyah and Lingah (on the Persian coast) simultaneously. He also flirted with the Egyptians during their Arabian expansionist period in the late 1830s and then supported the rival Al Bu SA'ID claimant to the Muscat throne, Qays bin 'Azzan. He was a party to the Treaty of Perpetual MARITIME PEACE in 1853 and died in April 1866 at the approximate age of 97.

SULTAN'S ARMED FORCES (SAF). The genesis of the Sultanate of OMAN's regular military capability came with the acquisition of BALUCHI levies under British leadership in 1921. First known as the MUSCAT Levy Corps, this group was later renamed the Muscat Infantry. Due to the demands made upon the 200-man group in the 1950s by the BURAYMI crisis, the security needs of oil exploration parties, and the insurgency of the OMAN REVOLUTIONARY MOVEMENT (ORM), additional troops were raised and organized into the Sultan's Armed Forces in 1958. The British assumed much of the responsibility for the force, including an operational subsidy from 1959 to 1967, and the seconding of some of its officers including the Commander (other officers have also been British but hired on private contract). Gradually other elements were added as the Sultanate of Oman's Navy and the Sultanate of Oman's Air Force. SAF began defensive operations in DHUFAR as early as 1965 but the main burden of the fighting there was carried by the independent Dhufar Force (at one time, all-Dhufari in its rank-and-file, with retired Pakistani officers and NCOs). But as the rebellion spread, the Dhufar Force was unable to handle the situation, whereupon SAF began to assume the responsibility, and the Dhufar Force was eventually absorbed into SAF. In the mid-1970s, SAF had over 12,000 personnel (about 70 per cent Arab and 30 Baluchi, the latter recruited both from Oman's BATINAH Coast and the Sultanate's former possession of GWADAR; previous to 1970, SAF was 70 per cent Baluchi). The headquarters--originally at BAYT al-FALAJ near MATRAH (scene of a 1915 tribal attack on Muscat)--were moved in the mid-1970s to Rusayl (near al-Sib International Airport). There are training missions at Ghalla and SAYQ as well as major field camps at al-RUSTAQ, SUHAR, NIZWA, Bidbid, IZKI and SALALAH.

SUMA'IL see WADI SAMA'IL

SUNNI. The main body or the orthodox sect of ISLAM. All other Islamic sects (such as the SHI'Is or IBADIs) have broken away from the Sunnis. Within Sunnism, there are four schools of interpretation of the SHARI'AH (Islamic law), which have contributed to the development of political factions in Eastern Arabia. Arabia itself has always been Sunni except for certain areas in al-BAHRAYN, OMAN, Yemen and SAUDI ARABIA.

SUQ (plural: aswaq). Arabic word for market, usually consisting of a group of small shops where local merchants sell any and all goods that the populace might require. There are suqs located in every village of any size. In the larger suqs of the coastal towns, Persian, Pakistani and Indian merchants will often be found, offering a wide variety of items for sale, such as pearls in al-BAHRAYN or gold and silver work in DUBAY and MATRAH. As in many other parts of the world, the suqs of Eastern Arabia are important gathering places for people of all classes, so much so that their reason for being at times seems as much social as commercial. For years, the most prosperous suqs in the area have been those of Dubay and al-Bahrayn.

SUR. The second largest seaport of the Sultanate of OMAN, Sur is located near RA'S al-HADD at the easternmost point of the Arabian Peninsula and is the only harbor of eastern Oman. It is also one of the oldest ports of the area and serves the JA'LAN and SHARQIYYAH hinterland. It has long been noted for its shipbuilding and seafaring (having been visited by the great Muslim traveler Ibn Battutah ca. 1324), as well as piracy and slave-running from the African coast. The town itself is located on an isthmus at the entrance to an inlet (except for the suburb of al-'Ayqah located on the mainland directly opposite). Another settlement called Bilad Sur, where the wali (governor) has his headquarters, is located several miles away along the track to the interior. Al-'Ayqah is inhabited by members of the Bani Bu 'ALI tribe while Sur itself is divided into four groups of the JANABAH (namely, al-Ghayalin, al-'Aramah, al-Mukhanah and al-Fuwaris). Although always nominally under the Sultanate, Sur has been noted for its xenophobia and independent spirit: it was bombarded several times in the 1920s by the British at the request of the Sultan because of continued disregard for his customs post. In the early 1970s a number of its inhabitants, including several women, were arrested and charged as being active supporters of the POPULAR FRONT FOR THE LIBERATION OF OMAN AND THE ARABIAN GULF. With medical clinics, housing, a modern school (named Ahmad bin Majid after the famous Arab navigator who is said to have been born and raised in Sur), construction underway of a paved road to the capital, and plans for developing its port facilities as an alternate to the busy harbor at MATRAH, Sur seemed destined in the mid-1970s to regain a measure of its earlier prominence in Omani affairs.

al-SUWAYQ. A settlement along the BATINAH Coast of OMAN, situated midway between al-MASNA'AH and al-KHABURAH. It is the territorial center of the Yal SA'D tribe and its inhabitants are mainly date cultivators and fishermen.

- T -

TOS see TRUCIAL OMAN SCOUTS

TALIB BIN 'ALI al-HINA'I. Brother of Imam GHALIB BIN 'ALI al-HINA'I (r. 1954-1955), Talib had been the long-time wali (governor) of al-RUSTAQ for the IMAMATE when his brother was elected Imam. Consequently, he became the dominant figure in the shortlived Imamate and was responsible for trying to expand its territory through the cash and arms that Saudi Arabia sent him through al-BURAYMI. When forces loyal to Sultan SA'ID BIN TAYMUR captured the interior of OMAN in late 1955, Talib fled to al-DAMMAM, Saudi Arabia, where he began to train the army of the OMAN REVOLUTIONARY MOVEMENT (ORM). Two years later in the summer of 1957, he and his men returned to Oman and revived the revolt. They were eventually repulsed and forced to flee into the JABAL al-AKHDAR from whence they escaped in early 1959, again to Saudi Arabia, then Egypt and finally Iraq. Talib subsequently appeared before the U. N. General Assembly to argue that the British had sponsored the "colony" of the "Sultanate of Muscat" against the "independent Imamate of Oman."

TAMIMAH (plural: tama'im). The Arabic term for paramount SHAYKH or a tribal leader who has control over all sections of his tribe and can count on their support in intertribal disputes. Not all tribes have tamimahs. The term is often technically defined as one who has the power to impose the death penalty on errant tribesmen.

TANUF. Formerly a settlement in OMAN province located at the base of the JABAL al-AKHDAR massif approximately halfway between NIZWA and BAHLA. It was the headquarters of the Bani RIYAM tribe and boasted a fortress belonging to the Riyami tamimah (paramount shaykh), SULAYMAN BIN HIMYAR. When a combined Sultanate of OMAN-British military force captured Tanuf after the revolt led by the OMAN REVOLUTIONARY MOVEMENT (ORM) in 1957, Sultan SA'ID BIN TAYMUR ordered it destroyed. The town has never been rebuilt.

TARIQ BIN TAYMUR AL BU SA'ID. Half-brother of the former Sultan of OMAN, SA'ID BIN TAYMUR (r. 1932-1970), and uncle of Sultan QABUS BIN SA'ID (r. 1970-), he was Prime Minister of the Sultanate of Oman in 1970-1971. Born in Istanbul and educated in Germany and India, he served with the Indian Army on the North-West Frontier before taking up permanent residence in Oman. He distinguished himself in action against the rebels of the OMAN REVOLUTIONARY MOVEMENT (ORM) in the 1950s but, not having been entrusted with a responsible position in the government by Sultan Sa'id, went into exile in 1962 and returned to Oman only after Qabus assumed the throne in 1970. In addition to holding the premiership during the first year following the 1970 coup d'état, he subsequently served as an advisor to the Ruler and as special emissary of the Sultan with the rank of ambassador. In 1976, Sultan Qabus, who had hitherto been a bachelor, married one of Tariq's daughters.

TAYMUR BIN FAYSAL AL BU SA'ID. Sultan of OMAN from 1913 to 1931. Taymur succeeded his father, FAYSAL BIN TURKI, in the midst of a tribal rebellion sparked by the election of an IBADI IMAM in 1913. The rebellion continued until Taymur signed the Agreement of al-SIB (1920) with leaders of the interior tribes, granting them a measure of autonomy. His reign saw the establishment of a Council of Ministers for the Sultanate in 1920 and the introduction of the forerunner of the SULTAN'S ARMED FORCES (SAF) in 1921, as well as the seconding of several British advisers to help in financial and military matters. Taymur was allowed to abdicate in favor of his son, SA'ID BIN TAYMUR, in 1931 and spent the rest of his life (d. 1965) in India, Japan and Singapore.

TELEGRAPH ISLAND [Jazirat al-Maqlab]. A small island in the middle of KHAWR al-SHAMM (Elphinstone Inlet) and neighbored by the larger Jazirat al-Shamm. Once suggested as the headquarters for the POLITICAL RESIDENCY IN THE PERSIAN GULF (PRPG), the island was used as a station for the INDO-EUROPEAN TELEGRAPH from 1864 to 1869, when it was abandoned as being too unhealthy a site after all three station managers died from malaria. A British flagstaff was erected on the island in 1904 (along with two others in the area) in an attempt to limit growing Russian influence in the GULF area but was never used.

THALER see MARIA THERESA THALER

THAMARIT (Midway). A point on the road from SALALAH to MUSCAT in the Sultanate of OMAN and located at the edge of the NAJD desert to the north of the QARA Mountains. During the DHUFAR REBELLION, control of Thamarit became a major military objective for both rebel and government forces, with the latter dominating the site from 1973 onwards. Until Raysut port was built in DHUFAR in the early 1970s, Salalah Plain was frequently cut off from the outside world by sea and air during the monsoon season--thus supplies had to be trucked in overland to Thamarit and then through the ambush-prone Qara Mountains to Salalah.

THANI, AL. The ruling family of the State of QATAR. The Al Thani were originally part of the widespread Bani Tamim tribe of central Arabia and arrived in Qatar in the early 17th century. They owed allegiance to the Al KHALIFAH family at al-ZUBARAH for a time and then became nominal vassals of the Ottoman Empire in the 19th century until the emirate became a British-protected state. Since in matters of religion the Al Thani are MUWAHHIDUN (Wahhabis), and tend to be conservative in other matters as well, they have traditionally enjoyed a close relationship with the ruling household in SAUDI ARABIA. Twentieth-century Rulers of Qatar who have come from the Al Thani include 'ABD ALLAH BIN QASIM (r. 1913-1949), 'ALI BIN 'ABD ALLAH (r. 1949-1960), AHMAD BIN 'ALI (r. 1960-1972) and KHALIFAH BIN HAMAD (r. 1972-). In addition, HAMAD BIN 'ABD ALLAH, father of the last of the aforementioned Rulers, had been heir apparent at his death in 1946.

THESIGER, WILFRED (b. 1910). British explorer of Southern and Eastern Arabia. Born in Addis Ababa and educated at Oxford, he became one of the first Europeans to explore the Danakil country of Abyssinia and later served in the Sudan Political Service. After World War II, he joined the Middle East Locust Control group and was sent to the Arabian Peninsula. Between 1945 and 1950 he made numerous journeys into and across the RUB' al-KHALI desert and came to know it like no other

Westerner before or since (he was the third to cross it after Bertram THOMAS in 1930-31 and H. St. John B. PHILBY in 1932). He wrote several professional articles describing his experiences and later consolidated them into Arabian Sands (London, 1959).

THOMAS, BERTRAM (1892-1950). A British explorer and government official, he was employed as financial adviser and WAZIR to the Sultanate of OMAN from 1925 to 1930 and later was Public Relations Officer in the Gulf during 1942 and 1943. During his employment in MUSCAT, he became the first European to cross the RUB' al-KHALI desert while gathering research on the area. His publications include Arabia Felix (London, 1932), Alarms and Excursions in Arabia (London, 1931), and several articles on the government of the Sultanate, the MUSANDAM PENINSULA and the South Arabian peoples of DHUFAR. He later became director of the Middle East Centre for Arabic Studies located in Palestine and then Lebanon.

THOMS, SHARON AND WELLS. American doctors and missionaries in the Sultanate of OMAN in the 20th century. Dr. Sharon Thoms opened the MATRAH Hospital of the ARABIAN MISSION (of the Reformed Church of America) in 1909 but died of injuries received in a fall in 1913. His son, Dr. Wells Thoms, came to Oman in 1939 and continued to head the Arabian Mission Hospital in Matrah until his retirement at the beginning of the 1970s. During most of their combined service of nearly forty years in Oman, the hospital they managed in MATRAH was one of only two extant in the Sultanate.

TOWELL, W. J., AND SONS. One of the largest trading firms in OMAN (with a branch in al-KUWAYT). Towell, the English founder, began the company in MATRAH in the 1860s. A later partner, Archibald McKirdy, also served as U. S. Vice-Consul in MUSCAT at the turn of the century. He was later succeeded in that position by his KHOJA partner, Muhammad Fadl, who acquired full ownership of the firm. In the mid-1970s, Fadl's family (under the name of Sultan) still controlled the firm.

TREATY OF PERPETUAL MARITIME PEACE see MARITIME PEACE, TREATY OF PERPETUAL

TRUCIAL COAST. The area covered by the States of ABU

DHABI, 'AJMAN, DUBAY, al-FUJAYRAH, RA'S al-KHAYMAH, SHARJAH and UMM al-QAYWAYN. The name comes from the Treaty of Perpetual MARITIME PEACE (1853) acceded to by the then five major shaykhs of the area. The treaty put an end to the periodic warfare on the surrounding sea that had plagued the area for so long. The accord also made the British guarantors of the peace and thus was an incipient stage in the evolution of these polities into British protected states, a status lasting until six of the seven states became independent in 1971, at which time they joined in the UNITED ARAB EMIRATES (UAE). Ra's al-Khaymah joined the federation in February 1972.

TRUCIAL OMAN LEVIES see TRUCIAL OMAN SCOUTS

TRUCIAL OMAN SCOUTS (TOS). Formed in 1951 at which time it was called the Trucial Oman Levies. This military force was established by Great Britain and generally used British officers on private contract and secondment. Its purpose was to provide security for oil company explorations and to prevent disputes between tribes and states from escalating into full-scale warfare. The TOS was instrumental in the eviction of the Saudi Arabian garrison from al-BURAYMI Oasis in 1955 and TOS detachments played a support role during the 1955-1959 rebellion in the Sultanate of OMAN by the OMAN REVOLUTIONARY MOVEMENT (ORM). When the seven states of the TRUCIAL COAST became independent in 1971, the TOS provided the nucleus of the new UNITED ARAB EMIRATES Defence Force.

TRUCIAL STATES see TRUCIAL COAST

TUNB ISLANDS. Greater and Lesser Tunb, two islands strategically located near the entrance to the GULF off the western coast of the UNITED ARAB EMIRATES. The islands were under the control of RA'S al-KHAYMAH until they were forcibly seized by the Iranian Navy on November 30, 1971. This act, along with the occupation of nearby ABU MUSA Island, continued to plague relations between Iran and the states on the Arab side of the Gulf through the mid-1970s.

\- U -

UAE see UNITED ARAB EMIRATES

'ULAMA' (singular: 'alim). Arabic term for theologians or religious scholars. In Eastern Arabia as elsewhere in the Islamic world, the 'ulama' are responsible for interpreting the SHARI'AH (Islamic law) and their interpretation varies according to which school of jurisprudence they follow. In modern times, their influence in a particular state has depended on the degree of secularization extant as well as which particular sect of Islam or school of jurisprudence predominates in that state. In the SHI'I sect, the term MULLAH is frequently substituted for 'alim, whereas the IBADI sect generally uses MUTAWWI'.

UMM. Arabic word meaning mother or source. In the latter sense it is sometimes part of a place name, as in UMM al-NAR.

UMM al-NAR. A small island of the State of ABU DHABI, located near the point where the Maqta' bridge connects Abu Dhabi Island with the mainland. It is noted for its prehistoric burial mounds, first excavated by a Danish archaeological team in the mid-1960s, which exhibited traces of a well-advanced civilization dating from 3000 B. C. More recently, the island has been the site of a fort manned by the TRUCIAL OMAN SCOUTS (now the United Arab Emirates Defence Force) and of an oil refinery built by the Abu Dhabi National Oil Co.

UMM al-QAYWAYN. One of the seven member states of the UNITED ARAB EMIRATES (UAE). Recognized as an independent shaykhdom by the British in the GENERAL TREATY OF PEACE in 1820, its leaders have been noted for their longevity; in the mid-1970s the Ruler was still Shaykh AHMAD BIN RASHID AL MU'ALLA (r. 1929-). The state has an area of 300 square miles with an estimated population of 17, 000, most of whom live in Umm al-Qaywayn Town (although there is a Qaywayni settlement around Falaj Al 'Ali in the HAJAR mountains behind the coast). The town is built across a saltwater inlet, as are neighboring capitals. The ruling household belongs to the Al 'Ali tribe. During the late 1960s and well into the 1970s the State was frequently at odds with the neighboring state of SHARJAH in a major dispute over the location of their off-shore boundary in an area where oil had been discovered.

UMM SA'ID. The major industrial site in the State of QATAR, located on the eastern coast of the Qatar Peninsula approximately 25 miles south of al-DAWHAH (Doha). It also serves as the country's major oil terminal, being connected to the DUKHAN oilfields on the Peninsula's western coast by a 50-mile pipeline. Umm Sa'id also has facilities for the refining and distribution of petroleum and its byproducts, fertilizer and gas liquefaction plants, and a floor mill and cement factory, which derive their power from the state's abundant natural gas resources that had previously been flared.

UMM al-SAMIM. The sabkhah (salt marsh) and area of quicksand located in western OMAN between the edge of the plateau of Oman Province and the sands of al-RUB' al-KHALI desert. In 1949 Wilfred THESIGER became the first European both to see and to cross the Umm al-Samim. In 1962, PETROLEUM DEVELOPMENT (OMAN) LTD. drilled a dry well in the northern part of the sabkhah. The area is often mined for salt by the DURU' tribe.

UMM al-ZAMUL. A small well in the RUB' al-KHALI at the point where the de facto territorial boundaries of SAUDI ARABIA, ABU DHABI and the Sultanate of OMAN meet, and whose sovereignty has long been a matter of dispute among the governments of these states.

'UMR, BANI (singular: Ma'muri). Tribe of the BATINAH province of OMAN, occupying the upper stretches of the Wadi al-Hawasinah and coastal areas around SUHAR and SHINAS. A GHAFIRI and IBADI tribe, they have traditionally been at odds with their neighbors, the HAWASINAH. Even so, both the Bani 'Umr and the Hawasinah have traditionally supplied many of the 'askaris (armed retainers) for the walis (governors) of the Sultanate of Oman. Until recently, they were nominally responsible for guarding the walls and gate of the town of MATRAH.

UNION DEFENCE FORCE see TRUCIAL OMAN SCOUTS; UNITED ARAB EMIRATES

UNITED ARAB EMIRATES (UAE). A federation of the seven states of ABU DHABI, DUBAY, SHARJAH, 'AJMAN, UMM al-QAYWAYN, RA'S al-KHAYMAH and al-FUJAYRAH. These states formerly constituted the TRUCIAL STATES and were all British protected states. With the official British withdrawal from the Gulf, these emirates received their full independence and decided to form the

UAE. Negotiations for such a political grouping began in Dubay in February 1968 between these seven states as well as al-BAHRAYN and QATAR. The last two emirates, however, chose to become independent states. The UAE came into existence with six members on December 2, 1971. Ra's al-Khaymah, the seventh member, joined in February 1972. The federation joined both the League of Arab States and the United Nations within a week of its founding. Shaykh ZAYID BIN SULTAN AL NUHAYYAN, the Ruler of Abu Dhabi, and Shaykh RASHID BIN SA'ID AL MAKTUM, the Ruler of Dubay, were elected to five-year terms as the federation's first President and Vice President, respectively. There is a constitution, a Federal National Council (FNC; consultative assembly) with 40 members chosen proportionately from the seven states and a Council of Ministers (or cabinet). In December 1973, the original 14-man Council of Ministers was doubled in size, and by the mid-1970s there were plans to increase the number of FNC deputies from 40 to 60. The former TRUCIAL OMAN SCOUTS (TOS) were transferred from British to UAE control at independence and were renamed Union Defence Force (UDF).

'URF. Arabic term meaning customary or tribal law. It is thus distinguished from SHARI'AH (Islamic law), which it antedates. The 'urf is steeped in the concept of collective responsibility rather than the completely individual responsibility of modern civil codes. Although the shari'ah has largely replaced 'urf in towns and cities, the latter remains an important regulator of badu (nomadic) life, involving such concepts as water rights and the blood feud. This is especially the case in some of the more remote regions of OMAN where the authority of the central government has only in recent years begun to take root.

UTUB, BANI (singular: 'Atbi). An important tribe of north-central Arabia, of which three branches settled in al-KUWAYT ca. 1716. One was the Al Sabah (which provided the ruling family of al-Kuwayt). The other two, the Al KHALIFAH and the Al Jalahimah, migrated to al-ZUBARAH on the QATAR Peninsula a half-century later, where they established a fishing and trading state. Eventually the Al Khalifah conquered the BAHRAYN Islands and provided the ruling family of a state founded there.

- W -

WADI (plural: awdiyah, or widyan). Arabic term for valley or watercourse. In Eastern Arabia, the wadis are generally dry and vary from a gently sloping dry watercourse such as the WADI HALFAYN to steep mountain canyons with permanent running water such as the WADI SAMA'IL. Other prominent wadis of the area are the WADI 'ANDAM and al-WADI al-JIZZI.

WADI 'ANDAM. One of the larger river beds of central OMAN, the Wadi 'Andam flows due south out of the eastern HAJAR Mountains and through al-SHARQIYYAH province until it merges with the WADI HALFAYN. The inhabitants along its course are principally from the Bani RUWAHAH tribe.

WADI HALFAYN. The major drainage route on the inland side of the HAJAR Mountains of OMAN. It begins at the divide where the WADI SAMA'IL (or Wadi Bani Ruwahah) slopes towards the GULF OF OMAN and continues in a southerly direction through IZKI and al-SHARQIYYAH province, being joined by the WADI 'ANDAM before disappearing in the WAHIBAH SANDS, not far from the Gulf of MASIRAH.

al-WADI al-JIZZI. A wadi bisecting the Western HAJAR mountain range of OMAN. That it has long been a major route between al-BURAYMI in the interior and SUHAR on the BATINAH Coast is due to its position as the only easily traversed path through the mountains between peninsular Oman in the north and the WADI SAMA'IL to the east. It was the scene of extensive copper mining in past millenia and attempts to rework existing mineral deposits were begun in the mid-1970s.

WADI SAMA'IL. The wadi that separates the eastern HAJAR Mountains from the western Hajar. It begins near IZKI and ends near the coast at al-SIB. There are several major settlements along its course, including Fanjah, Bidbid, al-Lajaylah, Sarur, and Upper and Lower Sama'il. The upper stretches of the wadi are known as Wadi Bani Ruwahah and the Bani RUWAHAH tribe dominates its course. The pipeline built by PETROLEUM DEVELOPMENT (OMAN) LTD. from FAHUD to the coast follows the wadi and as it is the major route from the coast to OMAN province, the fort at Sama'il has traditionally been the key to control of the interior. It is also one of the major centers of cultivation in Oman because of the relative abundance of water.

WAHHABI see MUWAHHIDUN

WAHIBAH, YAL (singular: Wahibi). One of the three great badu or nomadic tribes of OMAN, the Yal Wahibah is the only one that is IBADI; it belongs to the HINAWI political faction. The tribal dirah (territory) stretches from al-SHARQIYYAH province in the north to the Arabian Sea in the south, and from the WADI HALFAYN in the west to JA'LAN province in the east. In the south, Yal Wahibah are fishermen along the coast, but many migrate to harvest the date palms along the southern edges of the settled Sharqiyyah in the summer when the monsoon makes fishing impossible. Because of their "client" relationship with the HIRTH tribe during the ascendancy of AHMAD BIN MUHAMMAD al-HARITHI over much of the interior in the 1955-1970 period, the Yal Wahibah were able to extend the range of their dirah at the expense of the JANABAH, their major rivals, as well as gain added employment from PETROLEUM DEVELOPMENT (OMAN) LTD. A few have settled in other areas of Oman. The tribe should not be confused with the Bani Wahayb (singular, Wahaybi), who inhabit settlements in the Muscat district.

WAHIBAH SANDS. The sandy desert of OMAN which is bordered by al-SHARQIYYAH province on the north, the Arabian Sea on the south and east, and the UMM al-SAMIM and JIDDAT al-HARASIS desert on the west. It is almost as forbidding as the RUB' al-KHALI desert although not comparable in size and is inhabited solely by badu (nomads) of the Yal WAHIBAH.

WALI (plural: wulah). Arabic term for the representative of a ruler of a state in his outlying territory (wilayah--plural, wilayat--refers to the territory under the wali's control). In Eastern Arabia, the term is mostly employed in the Sultanate of OMAN. Generally, the wali is responsible for keeping the peace in the settlement to which he is assigned, although in some cases his authority may extend to surrounding territory (as in DHUFAR province or in areas where tribal authority is lacking). Normally, each wali is assisted by a qadi (Islamic judge) and in the Sultanate of Oman, the wali is responsible to the Ministry of the Interior in MUS-

CAT. The Sultanate assigns walis to the following settlements (as well as one for all of Dhufar province): BARKA, al-MASNA'AH, al-SUWAYQ, al-KHABURAH, SAHAM, SUHAR, LIWA, SHINAS (all in al-BATINAH province); KHASAB, DIBBA, and Bukha (in RU'US al-JIBAL); al-BURAYMI and Mahadah (in Jau and al-Buraymi region); DANK and 'IBRI (in al-DHAHIRAH province); BAHLA, NIZWA (with two deputy or na'ib walis), Birkat al-Mawz, Manah, and ADAM (in OMAN province); al-Mudaybi, Ibra, Wadi Bani Khalid, al-Mudayrib, and Bidiyyah (in al-SHARQIYYAH province); Bilad Bani Bu Hasan, Bilad Bani Bu 'Ali, al-Kamil and al-Wafi, Wadi Dimma, and SUR (in JA'LAN province); QURIYAT, Bidbid, SAMA'IL, and IZKI (in the Eastern HAJAR province); and NAKHL, Wadi al-Ma'awil, al RUSTAQ, and al-'Awabi (in the Western Hajar province). After the reorganization of government following the coup d'état of 1970, several schemes were advanced for the consolidation of these wilayahs on the lines of the geographical provinces but none had been utilized by the mid-1970s.

WALKER, JULIAN F. (b. 1929). British diplomat of the 20th century. Educated at Cambridge and the London School of Oriental and African Studies, he was appointed Assistant Political Agent in the TRUCIAL STATES (1953-1955) and then Third and Second Secretary to the POLITICAL RESIDENT IN THE PERSIAN GULF (1955-1957). From 1957 to 1960, he was involved in demarcating the complex boundaries of the Trucial States, being able to draw recognized frontiers in nearly two dozen of more than 30 disputed areas. After serving elsewhere for the Foreign Office, he returned to the area as Political Agent in DUBAY in 1971 (a position that was upgraded to Consul General and Counsellor in the British Embassy after Dubay became independent) and served there until 1972. As Political Agent in Dubay he was a key official in helping to secure the agreement of the then Trucial States rulers to form the UNITED ARAB EMIRATES.

WAZIR (plural: wuzara'). Arabic term for government minister. Traditionally it meant an individual who acted as a close adviser and/or confidant to the ruler of a state. Only recently have more formal administrative institutions been established in Eastern Arabia requiring proper ministers, ministries (wizarah), and heads of departments.

WELLSTED, J. R. A 19th-century officer of the Indian Navy. Along with Lt. F. Whitelock in 1835-36, he was the first European to travel in the interior of OMAN and to ascend the JABAL al-AKHDAR mountain range. His Travels in Arabia (London, 1838) recounts his experiences.

WHITELOCK, F. see WELLSTED, J. R.

WILAYAH see WALI

WILLIAMSON, WILLIAM (Hajji 'Abdullah). A 20th-century British personality of Arabia who converted to ISLAM and adopted the Arab way of life. Born in Bristol, Williamson became a sailor at a young age and set off to explore the world. He owned a ranch in California and was imprisoned in Manila for gun-running before joining the Aden Constabulary. He became a Muslim in Aden but subsequently left there as a result of official disapproval. He drifted to al-KUWAYT and made the pilgrimage to Mecca. Following this, he spent a period of time with the badu (nomadic) tribes of the NAJD (the central plateau of what is now SAUDI ARABIA), and then became a horse-dealer and gun-runner in the Gulf. During World War I, he served in the British Secret Service and after the war was recruited by Arnold Wilson as a guide and interpreter for the Anglo-Persian (later Anglo-Iranian) Oil Co. He was present on exploration parties to many areas of Eastern Arabia until his retirement to a southern Iraqi village in 1937.

WINGATE, SIR RONALD E. L. A 20th-century Government of India political official in the Gulf and son of one-time governor of the Sudan, Sir Reginald Wingate. After receiving his degree from Oxford University, he joined the Indian Political Service in 1912 and was posted to the Punjab and Mesopotamia before being transferred to MUSCAT as Political Agent in 1919. While there, he was responsible for bringing to an end the seven-year revolt by the Imamate of the interior by negotiating the Agreement of al-SIB (1920) between the Sultan and the interior shaykhs. He later served in Baluchistan and with the Foreign and Political Department of the Government of India, retiring in 1939.

- Y -

YA'AQIB (singular: Ya'qubi). An Omani tribe of al-DHAHIRAH province who dominate the town of 'IBRI. Like most of the other tribes of al-Dhahirah, they are SUNNI and GHAFIRI. Consequently, they were always opposed to the IBADI IMAMATE of interior OMAN and the town had to be forcibly subdued by the Imam's tribes. The re-occupation of 'Ibri by the Ibadis in 1954 after a rebellion of the Ya'aqib was a major factor in the occupation of the town by a military element of the Sultanate of OMAN. As is often the case elsewhere in Oman, the Ya'aqib exhibit a kind of "client" relationship over the principal badu (nomadic) tribe of the area, the DURU'.

al-YA'ARIBAH (singular: Ya'rubi). A small tribe of al-RUSTAQ and NAKHL whose fortunes have declined considerably since the 17th and 18th centuries, when it provided a dynasty of IBADI IMAMS for OMAN. The first of these Imams was Nasir bin Murshid who was elected at al-RUSTAQ in 1624 and proceeded to unite Oman and drive the Portuguese out of the country, only to die during the siege of the last Portuguese-held town at MUSCAT. He was succeeded by his cousin, Sultan bin Sayf, who did much to restore Oman's position in the world, following on the heels of the Portuguese withdrawal from areas along the coast of east Africa. This period established Oman as the predominant trading empire in Eastern Arabia and along the east African littoral. The dynasty was also responsible for building many of the impressive forts that dominate key Omani towns, such as at NIZWA, JABRIN and al-HAZM. Civil war broke out over the question of succession to the Imamate in the early 18th century and the outcome was two invasions of Oman by the Persians at the invitation of Ya'rubi contenders. The second invasion succeeded in capturing all of the coastline except SUHAR, whence the eventually successful revolt against the Persians began. As a result, the Ya'aribah tribe passed from prominence and its numbers were greatly reduced in inter-tribal fighting over the next two centuries.

YAL. Arabic term meaning family (probably a corruption of the classical <u>ayal</u>) and sometimes used as prefix to tribal names. For entries beginning with yal, see the individual name (e.g., WAHIBAH, YAL).

YAMANI see 'ADNANI-YAMANI DIVISION

YAS, BANI (singular: Yasi). One of the most important tribes in Eastern Arabia, the Bani Yas actually comprise a loose grouping of a number of small tribes. The original center of the tribe was in al-LIWA Oasis in what is now the western part of the State of ABU DHABI, which they share with the MANASIR tribe. Three major subdivisions of the tribe include the Al Bu FALAH (which founded Abu Dhabi Town in the mid-18th century and which includes the Al NUHAYYAN ruling family of Abu Dhabi); the Al Bu FALASAH (which split away from Abu Dhabi in the 1830s and founded DUBAY Town, and which includes the Al MAKTUM dynasty of Dubay); and the Qubaysat (a coastal group that on several occasions in the 19th century unsuccessfully attempted to secede from Abu Dhabi and settle at KHAWR al-'UDAYD). Other major units include the Rawashid, Mazari', SUDAN and Al Bu Muhayr. Bani Yas tribesmen are not confined to Abu Dhabi and Dubay but are found throughout the UNITED ARAB EMIRATES, as well as in the Sultanate of OMAN, QATAR and al-BAHRAYN.

YEMEN/YEMENI see 'ADANI-YAMANI DIVISION

- Z -

al-ZAFRAH see al-DHAFRAH

ZAHIR BIN GHUSN al-HINA'I. An important tamimah (paramount shaykh) of the Bani HINA who ruled the tribe in the first part of the 20th century. Zahir bin Ghusn was responsible for extending the influence of the tribe as a force to be reckoned with in OMAN province. His eight sons (the Awlad Zahir) have also played an important part in 20th-century Omani history. 'Abd Allah has been the tamimah of the tribe for the past quarter-century, Muhammad has been wali (governor) of SAMA'IL for the last decade, 'Ali has been wali of al-Mudaybi in al-SHARQIYYAH province, and al-Walid became first Minister of Education, then of Awqaf and Islamic Affairs, under Sultan QABUS BIN SA'ID. Another brother died in Jalali Prison in MUSCAT, where he was incarcerated for his role in the 1950s rebellion. Important cousins to the Awlad Zahir are the former Imam GHALIB BIN 'ALI al-HINA'I and his brother TALIB.

al-ZAHIRAH see al-DHAHIRAH

ZAKAT. The Islamic alms-tax which is one of the five fundamental obligations of every Muslim and is variably levied on production. As state and religion were inseparable in early Islam, the zakat has continued to be collected at least periodically by the states of Eastern Arabia. SAUDI ARABIAN claims to al-BURAYMI and other parts of Eastern Arabia (including areas in the Sultanate of Oman) have relied on the record of previous forced collections of zakat from inhabitants of the area. Originally used as a principal source for aiding the poor, the widowed, the orphaned and the disabled, the importance of zakat has diminished in recent years owing to the much greater largesse available for social welfare programs in general through the accumulation of revenues from petroleum production.

ZANZIBAR. A group of islands off the coast of East Africa, the most important being Zanzibar and Pemba, and now forming part of the Republic of Tanzania. Zanzibar has long had links with Eastern Arabia through centuries of trade via the DHOW traffic between Arabia and Africa and vice versa. The Arab influence was interrupted by Persian colonization in the 10th century and by Portuguese domination in the 16th and 17th centuries. With OMAN's independence from Portugal, Omani control was reasserted over Zanzibar and the East African littoral. This control was very loose, however, until SA'ID BIN SULTAN AL BU SA'ID became Sultan of Oman in 1807. Over the next four decades, Sa'id increased his domination of the East African coast and interior and eventually made Zanzibar his permanent residence. On his death, his son Majid ruled Zanzibar independently of Oman (his reign was confirmed by the CANNING AWARD of 1861) and the Al Bu SA'ID family established a century-long dynasty there. Britain established a protectorate over the Sultanate of Zanzibar in 1890 that lasted until independence in 1963. A few months later, a black African nationalist revolution broke out and many Arabs were killed. The Sultan fled to England and a number of Arabs resettled in the Gulf. Zanzibar has had a significant impact on Omani politics over the last century. Many Omani tribesmen emigrated to Zanzibar, individually or by family, some remaining for only a few years and then returning to Oman. This mobility was especially true of the inhabitants of the SHARQIYYAH province of Oman. For these and other Omanis, their African destination was not limited to Zanzibar but extended in many instances to much of the East

African mainland, including Tanzania, Kenya and the Congo. Until Zanzibar became a protectorate, its Sultans frequently intrigued against the Omani Sultans: in the Oman rebellion during World War I, German intrigues among the rebels were thought to have originated from Zanzibar and German East Africa (now Tanzania). Even today, Swahili is a frequently heard language in al-SHARQIYYAH.

ZANZIBAR SUBSIDY. The Zanzibar Subsidy dates from the CANNING AWARD of 1861, by which Oman and Zanzibar were officially recognized by the Government of India as separate states. Since Zanzibar was the more prosperous portion, the Government of India decreed that the Sultan of Zanzibar should pay the Sultan of OMAN an annual sum of 86,400 rupees to equalize the income of the two parts. Within a few years, the sultans of Zanzibar refused to pay the subsidy and it was assumed by the Government of India. Oman continued to receive the sum as a direct subsidy until 1970, when it was discontinued because of the influx of oil revenues.

ZAYID BIN KHALIFAH AL NUHAYYAN (the Great). The 19th-century Ruler of ABU DHABI. He succeeded his cousin, Sa'id bin Tahnun, in 1855 and a few years later successfully defended Abu Dhabi against a combined attack by Sa'id and the QASIMI dynasty of SHARJAH. In 1870, he allied himself with the IMAM of OMAN, 'AZZAN BIN QAYS AL BU SA'ID, in order to drive the SAUDIS from al-BURAYMI oasis and al-DHAFRAH region. By the late 1890s, alliances with the NA'IM tribe and war against the DHAWAHIR tribe allowed Zayid to gain control of the Buraymi village of al-'AYN, which has continued to remain in the possession of Abu Dhabi (except for Saudi occupation in 1952-1955). Zayid thwarted an attempt by the Qubaysat section of the Al Bu FALAH to secede from Abu Dhabi and create an independent state at KHAWR al-'UDAYD. He received British support in this endeavor and in a subsequent war with QATAR because of the Turkish influence over Qatar. He died of natural causes in 1909, the most respected ruler of the TRUCIAL COAST.

ZAYID BIN SULTAN AL NUHAYYAN. Ruler of ABU DHABI (r. 1966-) and President of the UNITED ARAB EMIRATES (UAE) since its inception in 1971. He had been the governor of al-'AYN (the main Abu Dhabi village in al-BURAYMI oasis complex) when it was occupied by a

Saudi garrison in the early 1950s. He became Ruler of Abu Dhabi in 1966 when his brother, SHAKHBUT BIN SULTAN, was deposed (with British approval) as a result of his inability or unwillingness to disburse effectively the increasing revenues accruing to the state from oil production. Under Shaykh Zayid's leadership, Abu Dhabi grew into a modern metropolis, and Zayid acquired a reputation for generosity in financial aid and successful statesmanship, particularly in the settlement of border disputes, with respect to which, in the mid-1970s, he was without a peer in Eastern Arabia.

ZATUT (singular: Zutti). A non-Arab OMAN tribe of unknown origin. Its members have variously been called a branch of the Saluba tribe of northern Arabia (whose non-Arab origins are likewise shrouded in mystery), gypsies, and ancient immigrants from India. They occupy a low-caste position in Omani society. Not being allowed to settle in tribal territory, they have tended to inhabit larger settlements such as al-BURAYMI and MATRAH/MUSCAT. Despite the disdain with which many of the Arab inhabitants have traditionally regarded them, they play an important economic role through their metalwork and carpentry, as well as their skill in performing circumcisions.

ZAWAHIR see DHAWAHIR

ZIKI see IZKI

al-ZUBARAH. A settlement on the northwest coast of the QATAR Peninsula. The Al KHALIFAH family (the ruling household of al-BAHRAYN) migrated to al-Bahrayn from this village ca. 1783. Well into this century the NA'IM inhabitants of al-Zubarah proclaimed their allegiance to the Al Khalifah--a factor behind al-Bahrayn's longstanding claim to sovereignty over the settlement. This contention has been vigorously denied by Qatar. Although the disputed claim remained a source of tension between the two states, there were no signs in the mid-1970s that the matter was anywhere near resolution.

ZUFAR see DHUFAR

ZWEMER, PETER AND SAMUEL. American missionaries of the late 19th and early 20th centuries. Samuel helped establish the ARABIAN MISSION of the Reformed Church of America in the late 19th century and wrote a number of books on religion, missionary activities and the Middle East. His son Peter was the first member of the Arabian Mission to be stationed in MUSCAT (in 1891) and in 1896 he visited the JABAL al-AKHDAR, being one of two Westerners to do so between 1837-1959. Peter died in 1898 of malaria contracted in Muscat.

SELECT BIBLIOGRAPHY

This brief bibliography is recommended to both the general reader and the specialist in search of further knowledge and understanding of any of the topics and themes treated here. The selected publications of the authors cited therein, to which the contributors to this dictionary acknowledge their debt, constitute a rich and informative body of literature that is often overlooked by students of the area. They are recommended especially for the insight they afford into the attitudes, values, customs, life styles, political and socio-economic systems and overall culture of the people of Eastern Arabia.

BIBLIOGRAPHIES

Anthony, John Duke. *The States of the Arabian Peninsula and the Gulf Littoral: A Selected Bibliography.* Washington, D. C.: Middle East Institute, 1973.

The Arabian Peninsula: A Selective, Annotated List of Periodicals, Books and Articles in English. Washington, D. C.: Library of Congress, 1951 (reprinted, New York: Greenwood Press, 1968).

Atiyah, George N., comp. *The Contemporary Middle East, 1948-1973: A Selective and Annotated Bibliography.* Boston: G. K. Hall, 1975.

Geddes, Charles L. *Analytical Guide to the Bibliographies on the Arabian Peninsula.* Denver: American Institute of Islamic Studies, 1974. (Bibliographic Series no. 4.)

Kabeel, Soraya. *Selected Bibliography on Kuwait and the Arabian Gulf.* Kuwait: Libraries Dept. of Kuwait University, 1969.

Macro, Eric. Bibliography of the Arabian Peninsula. Coral Gables, Fla.: University of Miami Press, 1958.

GENERAL

Anthony, John Duke. Arab States of the Lower Gulf: People, Politics, Petroleum. Washington, D.C.: Middle East Institute, 1975.

________. "The Arabian/Persian Gulf in Regional and International Politics: The Arab Side of the Gulf," in New Perspectives on the Persian Gulf, Hearings of the Subcommittee on the Near East, Committee on International Relations, U.S. House of Representatives (Washington, D.C.: U.S. Gov. Printing Office, 1973).

________. "The Impact of Oil on Political and Socioeconomic Change in the United Arab Emirates," in J. D. Anthony, ed., The Middle East: Oil, Politics, and Development (Washington, D.C.: American Enterprise Institute for Public Policy Research, 1975).

________. "Insurrection and Intervention: The War in Dhufar," in Abbas Amirie, ed. The Persian Gulf and Indian Ocean in International Politics (Teheran: Institute for International Political and Economic Studies, 1975), pp. 287-303.

________. "The Lower Gulf States: New Roles in Regional Affairs," in New Perspectives on the Persian Gulf, Hearings of the Subcommittee on the Near East, Committee on International Relations, U.S. House of Representatives (Washington, D.C.: U.S. Gov. Printing Office, 1973.

________. "The Union of Arab Amirates." Middle East Journal, vol. 26, no. 3 (1972).

Badger, Rev. G. P. History of the Imams and Seyyids of 'Oman, by Salil ibn Razik. London: Hakluyt Society, 1871.

al-Baharna, Husain. The Arabian Gulf States: Their Legal and Political Status and Their International Problems, 2nd ed. Beirut: Librairie du Liban, 1975.

Belgrave, Sir Charles D. Personal Column. London: Hutchinson, 1960 (reprinted, Beirut: Librairie du Liban, 1972).

________. The Pirate Coast. London: Bell, 1966 (reprinted, Beirut: Librairie du Liban, 1972).

Belgrave, James H. D. Welcome to Bahrain, 8th ed. al-Manamah: Augustan Press, 1973.

Bent, J. Theodore, and Mabel V. A. Southern Arabia. London: Smith, Elder and Co., 1900.

Boustead, Sir Hugh. The Wind of Morning. London: Chatto and Windus, 1972.

Bowen, Richard Le Baron, Jr. "The Arab Dhow Sailor." American Neptune, vol. 11, no. 3 (1951), 5-46.

________. "Arab Dhows of Eastern Arabia." American Neptune, vol. 9 (1949), 87-132.

________. "Marine Industries of Eastern Arabia." Geographical Review, vol. 41, no. 3 (1951), 384-400.

________. "The Pearl Fisheries of the Persian Gulf." Middle East Journal, vol. 5, no. 2 (1951), 161-80.

________. "Primitive Watercraft in Arabia." American Neptune, vol. 12 (1952), 186-221.

Brinton, Jasper Y. "The Arabian Peninsula: The Protectorates and the Sheikhdoms." Revue egyptienne de droit international, vol. 3 (1947), 25-38.

Busch, Briton Cooper. Britain and the Persian Gulf, 1894-1914. Berkeley: University of California Press, 1967.

Dickson, Harold Richard Patrick. The Arab of the Desert. London: George Allen and Unwin, 1949.

________. Kuwayt and Its Neighbours. London: George Allen and Unwin, 1956.

Dowson, V. H. W. "The Date and the Arab." Journal of the Royal Central Asian Society, vol. 36, pt. 1 (1949), 34-41.

Edo, Michael E. "Arabian Currency Arrangements Seen Evolving in Context of Rapid Change." IMF Survey, Dec. 9, 1974.

_______. "Character of Currencies of Arabian Peninsula Shaped by Recent Origin, Area's Resources." IMF Survey, Jan. 6, 1975.

Falcon, N. L. "The Musandam (Northern Oman) Expedition, 1971/1972." The Geographical Journal, vol. 139, pt. 1 (1973), 1-18.

Faris, Nabih A. "Derivation and Orthography of al-Rub' al-Khali." Journal of the Royal Central Asian Society, vol. 44, pt. 1 (1957), 28-30.

Fenelon, Kevin G. The United Arab Emirates: An Economic and Social Survey. London: Longman, 1973.

Great Britain. Memorial of the Government of the United Kingdom of Great Britain and Northern Ireland in Arbitration Concerning Buraimi and the Common Frontier Between Abu Dhabi and Saudi Arabia. 2 vols. London: HMSO, 1955.

Green, Timothy. The World of Gold. New York: Simon and Schuster, 1968.

Hawley, Donald. The Trucial States. London: George Allen and Unwin; New York: Twayne Publishers, 1970.

Hay, Sir Rupert. The Persian Gulf States. Washington, D.C.: Middle East Institute, 1959.

Heard-Bey, Frauke. "Development Anomalies in the Bedouin Oases of al-Liaw." Asian Affairs, vol. 61, pt. 3 (1974), 272-86.

_______. "Social Change in the Gulf States and Oman." Asian Affairs, vol. 59, pt. 1 (1972), 14-22; pt. 3, 309-16.

Hopwood, Derek, ed. The Arabian Peninsula: Society and Politics. London: George Allen and Unwin, 1972.

Kelly, John B. Britain and the Persian Gulf, 1795-1880. Oxford: Oxford University Press, 1968.

_______. Eastern Arabian Frontiers. London: Faber and Faber; New York: Praeger, 1964.

_______. "The Legal and Historical Basis of the British Position in the Persian Gulf." Middle Eastern Affairs, no. 1 (St. Antony's Papers, no. 4.)

Khadduri, Majid. "Iran's Claim to the Sovereignty of Bahrayn." American Journal of International Law, vol. 45 (1951), Supplements, 631-47.

_______. "Other Territorial and Jurisdictional Issues," in Majid Khadduri, ed., Major Middle Eastern Problems of International Law (Washington, D.C.: American Enterprise Institute, 1972).

Landen, Robert G. Oman Since 1856: Disruptive Modernization in a Traditional Arab Society. Princeton, N.J.: Princeton University Press, 1967.

Liebesny, Herbert J. "Administrative and Legal Development in Arabia: The Persian Gulf Principalities." Middle East Journal, vol. 10, no. 1 (1956), 33-42.

_______. "British Jurisdiction in the States of the Persian Gulf." Middle East Journal, vol. 3, no. 3 (1949), 330-32.

_______. "International Relations of Arabia: The Dependent States." Middle East Journal, vol. 1, no. 2 (1947), 148-68.

_______. "Legislation on the Sea-Bed and Territorial Waters of the Persian Gulf." Middle East Journal, vol. 4, no. 1 (1950), 94-96.

Longrigg, Stephen H. Oil in the Middle East: Its Discovery and Development, 3rd ed. Oxford: Oxford University Press, 1968.

Lorimer, John G. Gazetteer of the Persian Gulf, 'Oman and Central Arabia. Calcutta: Government of India, 1908, 1915 (reprinted, Farnborough, Hampshire: Gregg International, 1970).

El Mallakh, Ragaei. "Abu Dhabi: The Challenge of Affluence." Middle East Journal, vol. 24, no. 2 (1970), 135-46.

_______. "Economic Requirements for Development: Oman."

Middle East Journal, vol. 26, no. 4 (1972), 415-28.

Mann, Clarence. Abu Dhabi, Birth of an Oil Sheikhdom. Beirut: Khayats, 1964.

Melamid, Alexander. "The Buraimi Oasis Dispute." Middle Eastern Affairs, vol. 7, no. 2 (1956), 56-63.

________. "Oil and the Evolution of Boundaries in Eastern Arabia." Geographical Review, vol. 44 (Aug. 1954), 295-96.

________. "Political Geography of Trucial Oman and Qatar." Geographical Review, vol. 43, no. 2 (1953), 194-206.

________. "Transportation in Eastern Arabia." Geographical Review, vol. 52, no. 1 (1962), 122-24.

Mertz, Robert Anton. Education and Manpower in the Arabian Gulf. Washington, D.C.: American Friends of the Middle East, 1972.

Miles, Samuel B. The Countries and Tribes of the Persian Gulf. London: Harrison and Sons, 1919 (reprinted, London: Frank Cass, 1966).

Oman, Sultanate of. Oman. Muscat: Department of Information, 1972.

Palgrave, William G. Narrative of a Year's Journey through Central and Eastern Arabia. London: Macmillan and Co., 1865 (reprinted, Farnborough, Hampshire: Gregg International, 1969).

Peterson, John Everett. "The Revival of the Ibadi Imamate in Oman and the Revolt of 1913-1920." Arabian Studies, vol. 3 (1976).

Price, D. L. "Oman: Insurgency and Development." Conflict Studies, no. 53 (Jan. 1975).

Qubain, Fahim. "Social Classes and Tensions in Bahrain." Middle East Journal, vol. 9, no. 3 (1955), 269-80.

Ramazani, Rouhollah K. The Persian Gulf: Iran's Role. Charlottesville: University Press of Virginia, 1972.

________. "The Settlement of the Bahrain Question." Indian Journal of International Law, vol. 12, no. 1 (Jan. 1972).

Rentz, George, et al. The Eastern Reaches of al-Hasa Province. Dhahran, Saudi Arabia: Arabian American Oil Co., 1950.

________. Oman and the Southern Shores of the Persian Gulf. Cairo: n.p., 1952.

Ross, Edward C. "Annals of 'Oman, from Early Times to the Year 1728 A.D.," Journal of the Asian Society of Bengal, vol. 43 (1874).

Sadik, Muhammad T., and William P. Snavely. Bahrain, Qatar and the United Arab Emirates: Colonial Past, Present Problems and Future Prospects. Lexington, Mass.: Lexington Books, 1972.

Saudi Arabia. Memorial of the Government of Saudi Arabia in the Arbitration for the Settlement of the Territorial Dispute between Muscat and Abu Dhabi on One Side and Saudi Arabia on the Other. Cairo: n.p., 1955.

Skeet, Ian. Muscat and Oman: The End of an Era. London: Faber and Faber, 1974.

Stanford Research Institute. The Peripheral States of the Arabian Peninsula. Area Handbook prepared for the American University. Washington, D.C.: U.S. Gov. Printing Office, 1971.

Thesiger, Wilfred P. Arabian Sands. London: Longman: New York: Dutton, 1959.

Thomas, Bertram S. Alarms and Excursions in Arabia. London: George Allen and Unwin, 1931.

________. "Among Some Unknown Tribes of South Arabia." Journal of the Royal Anthropological Institute, vol. 49 (1929), 97-111.

________. "Four Strange Tongues from South Arabia--the Hadara Group." Proceedings of the British Academy, vol. 23 (1937).

________. "The Musandam Peninsula and Its People the

Shihuh." Journal of the Royal Central Asian Society, vol. 16, pt. 1 (1929), 71-86.

Wellsted, J. R. Travels in Arabia. London, 1838.

Wilkinson, John C. "Bayasirah and Bayadir." Arabian Studies I, pp. 75-85.

________. The Organization of the Falaj Irrigation System in Oman. Oxford: School of Geography, University of Oxford, July 1974. (Research Paper no. 10.)

Wilson, Sir Arnold T. The Persian Gulf: An Historical Sketch from the Earliest Times to the Beginning of the Twentieth Century. London: George Allen and Unwin, 1928.